"*UnClobber* is a breath of fresh air in the often swampy religious conversations on h̶   'WS

"Funny, smart, and bril   tten *that* book. The one you   who knows that inclusion is the only path forward but keeps getting told, 'but the Bible says. . . .' In his fresh and accessible way, Martin shows what the Bible actually says—clearing up all sorts of confusion along the way."
        —ROB BELL, *New York Times*
        best-selling author of *Love Wins*

"Thousands of sincere evangelical Christians feel a deep tension between their head and their heart. In their heads, they understand the Bible (and God) as the uncompromising enemy of LGBTQ people. But in their hearts, they find it hard to condemn or exclude them. Some people tell them to choose their heart over their head; others say the reverse. Colby Martin's highly readable and deeply engaging new book, *UnClobber*, offers a third option: a different way of aligning head and heart through a fresh look at Scripture. Written with a theologian's intelligence and a pastor's sensitivity, this book is the resource thousands have been waiting for."
        —BRIAN D. McLAREN, author and activist

"Martin takes a compassionate and scholarly look at the Scriptures on same-sex relationships that so many Christians have camped on and provides an accessible new framework that extends affirmation and inclusion to the LGBTQ community. *UnClobber* combines thoughtful theological study with a compelling pastoral memoir to create a powerful progressive Christian manifesto. This is a call for *all* Christians to love better and without condition."
        —KRISTEN HOWERTON, author
        of *Rage against the Minivan*

"If you've ever wondered what the Bible really says about homosexuality, you need to read this book. Martin doesn't work around the 'Clobber Passages" but faces them head on. He not only shows us that he's a thoughtful theologian but also perfectly displays the beauty of his humanness by sharing vulnerably about his own story in the only way he knows how: with honesty, humor, and grace. A profoundly important book!"

—CANDICE CZUBERNAT, therapist, writer, and founder of The Christian Closet

"This is a poignant and moving memoir of a pastor who lost his job to find grace-filled community, and a deep and incisive survey of the "Clobber Passages" of the Bible. Colby Martin's *UnClobber* is a compelling and profound journey that draws both heart and mind deeper into the Kingdom of God."

—RICHARD BECK, author, blogger, and professor of psychology at Abilene Christian University

"This is a unique book, written by a special author. Martin's insight, winsome spirit, and passion have come together to create a book that I not only love but am proud to share with those whom I love. *UnClobber* is a great gift for all who are seeking deeper understanding, faith, and compassion."

—DOUG PAGITT, pastor, author, and cofounder of Vote Common Good

UnClobber

Expanded Edition with Study Guide

UnClobber

Rethinking Our Misuse of the Bible on Homosexuality

Expanded Edition with Study Guide

COLBY MARTIN

WESTMINSTER JOHN KNOX PRESS
LOUISVILLE · KENTUCKY

First edition
Published by Westminster John Knox Press
Louisville, Kentucky

24 25 26 27 28 29 30 31 — 10 9 8 7 6 5 4

Book design by Drew Stevens
Cover design by Barbara LeVan Fisher/levanfisherstudio.com

Library of Congress Cataloging-in-Publication Data
Names: Martin, Colby, author.
Title: Unclobber : rethinking our misuse of the Bible on homosexuality / Colby Martin.
Description: Expanded edition with study guide. I Louisville : Westminster John Knox Press, [2022] I Summary: "Reexamines what the Bible says (and does not say) about homosexuality by looking at the six "Clobber Passages" that are frequently used by conservative Christianity to stand against full LGBTQ inclusion"-- Provided by publisher.
Identifiers: LCCN 2021057658 (print) I LCCN 2021057659 (ebook) I ISBN 9780664267469 (paperback) I ISBN 9781646982431 (ebook)
Subjects: LCSH: Homosexuality--Biblical teaching.
Classification: LCC BS680.H67 M37 2022 (print) I LCC BS680.H67 (ebook) I DDC 220.8/306766--dc23/eng/20220104
LC record available at https://lccn.loc.gov/2021057658
LC ebook record available at https://lccn.loc.gov/2021057659

PRINTED IN THE UNITED STATES OF AMERICA

♾ The paper used in this publication meets the minimum requirements of the American National Standard for Information Sciences — Permanence of Paper for Printed Library Materials, ANSI Z39.48-1992.

Most Westminster John Knox Press books are available at special quantity discounts when purchased in bulk by corporations, organizations, and special-interest groups. For more information, please e-mail SpecialSales@wjkbooks.com.

To Kate,
the fiercest, most inspiring warrior I know.
You have simultaneously softened me
and made me stronger than ever.
Thank you for the front row seat
to witness unconditional love.
An adventure, my love?
Always, my love.

CONTENTS

→

FOREWORD

Scripture tells that we are to work out our faith with fear and trembling. In practice, this is incredibly difficult.

And since life is already hard, we prefer our faith to be easy. We want to go to church on Sunday for a break—to sit back and (mostly) listen to our leaders. If our leaders teach something that feels off tune or insults our souls or other members of our human family—something that seems to fly in the face of the God of love—it's tempting to let it go. Too afraid to rock the boat, too tired to wrestle, we don't raise our hands. We sit quietly and tune out, or do one of those silent, internal eye rolls.

That silence is a really big deal.

That silence forms the future of the church.

Our children and our friends can't see our internal discomfort. To them, our quiet translates as agreement. And we've missed our chance: to change, to do a *new thing*. God is always, always trying to do a new thing. And those twinges of discomfort are God's invitations to cocreate. Our refusal to wrestle, to engage, to challenge is our refusal to cocreate with God.

The most repeated phrase in the Bible is "fear not." And so, when we feel that something we are hearing doesn't resonate with the God of love, we must raise our hands.

Even—especially—if our hands shake with fear and trembling. Apathy and passivity are the opposite of love. When we stay silent, we are making a big, bold decision. We are casting a loud vote for the status quo. It's a vote for fear over love. And the only thing necessary for the triumph of discrimination in the Christian faith is for doubtful Christians to stay quiet.

Colby Martin is one of my favorite hand-raisers. Colby's doubt that the will of God and the will of his human leaders were one and the same led him on a journey that took him into the desert and then toward the promised land. Colby saw that a whole lot of folks are trying harder to be good Christians than to be like Jesus—a tricky proposition because the world's definition of a good Christian is ever-changing. So Colby decided to quit trying to be a good Christian and start being like Jesus, and that has made all the difference because Jesus doesn't change. Jesus forever finds the outcast and brings her to the head of the table, invites her to lead. Jesus is the still, small voice forever leading us back to the truth—toward grace and love for all.

Even when Jesus called Colby away from his fold, away from safety and security (doesn't he always?), Colby went. With the encouragement and bravery of his warrior wife, Kate, he followed. And he took God and his incredible mind for Scripture with him. And—alone with Jesus and Kate—Colby deepened his understanding of Scripture and love. The deeper it got, the wider it got (doesn't it always?), until it included everybody.

Everybody's in, baby.

Colby doesn't play it safe. He dives right into the deep end—into the scary, wonderful, messy truth of a grace free for all.

UnClobber is the memoir of a brave, vulnerable, honest, beautiful couple's dance with the God of the outcast; it is also a sharp, fresh, wise take on Scripture. *UnClobber* will free its readers to love bigger and better and wiser.

As for Colby—I am so grateful that after a long road, this prophet has finally found a place to rest his fully human, absolutely divine head.

I have a feeling he has only just begun to love.

Glennon Doyle
March 2016

INTRODUCTION

---→

THE ORIGIN OF
UNCLOBBER

UnClobber . . . Did You Make That Up?

Why yes, yes, I did. Which made it that much easier to trademark.

UnClobber is my attempt to say, in one word, that I do not believe that God stands opposed to those who are attracted to the same sex or that God withholds divine blessing from a same-sex relationship. *UnClobber* came out of my desire to reverse the damage of the so-called "Clobber Passages."

At some point within the past few decades, the term "Clobber Passage" was coined because, well, I imagine being told that you are an abomination destined for the fires of hell and responsible for catastrophes like earthquakes and AIDS is probably a feeling similar to being clobbered over the head with a large object. There are approximately six verses (out of 31,000) in Scripture that appear to reference same-sex sex acts, and our gay brothers, sisters, and siblings have long felt the brunt of these six verses as the Christian church has historically used them to deny the LGBTQ community a seat at the Table of God, as full recipients of grace, and as full participants in the body of Christ.

So I want to UnClobber those who identify as gay, lesbian, transgender, bisexual, or queer. I want them to hear a different voice. One that says, "You are loved just as you are, by God and by me." But it's not just me, because there are millions of Christians around the world who are desperate for their gay loved ones to know that we see them, we believe in them, and we have their backs. I want them to hear that the Bible does not condemn them, as they've been led to believe. I want them to hear that their spot at the Table is open, it has been reserved for them, and, in fact, it's probably a chair or two closer to where Jesus is sitting because of all the unwarranted persecution they have endured at the hands of churches, pastors, and Christian organizations.

I want to them to hear a better story so that they can live a better story.

Speaking of Story . . .

In addition to unpacking the Clobber Passages, I want to tell you part of my story.

It's a story of how I found alignment between my head and my heart regarding the Bible and homosexuality. But beyond that, once those two realties lined up, it launched me to a more expansive journey of seeking that head-heart alignment in my ministry as a pastor and, indeed, my life as a whole. While my inner convictions were heading in one direction, my vocational situation remained entrenched in a more conservative evangelical environment.

This book, then, is about seeking a faith community where I could be a pastor who studies the Scriptures, worships and follows Jesus, recites the ancient creeds, builds authentic relationships between people from all walks of life, and opens the doors to welcome, affirm, and celebrate the LGBTQ community.

Part of my story involves some difficult truth-telling as I talk about the challenges I faced coming out as a straight ally. It was not a popular move. But my goal is not to shame or judge those who felt differently and who did harm to me in the process. Rather, I want to be honest about what I've gone through in my pursuit of an aligned life. To that end, if I felt that a particular story does not edify the person or place in question, I have changed their names for the sake of anonymity.

Where Did *UnClobber* Come From?

In a handful of videos on YouTube, I engage the topic of homosexuality in the Bible. One in particular has more than four hundred comments on it, which are split fairly evenly between supportive encouragement and hell-fire damnation. Here is a quote from one person who commented recently: "Colby, [you say] you studied the Bible and could not find God's Holy Word to be against homosexual sin? Are you kidding me? The Bible is crystal clear on same sex unions. You must have missed these verses . . ." He/She/It (unsurprisingly, the commenter was anonymous) goes on to copy and paste the "Clobber Passages."

This is not the first time I've received a reaction like this, nor will it be the last (more on that in chapter 10). For many non-affirming Christians, the Bible appears so clear on its stance toward homosexuality that the only reasonable conclusion is that affirming Christians, like myself, "must have missed" verses. I've written this book, in part, to show that I, and others like me, have surely not missed any verses.

When I came out of the theological closet, I began dialoguing with friends on Facebook about my new beliefs. Inevitably, people asked about my take on the "Clobber Passages." It wasn't long before I realized that Facebook threads are not the best format for exploring controversial Bible verses, so I told everyone to wait while I composed a series of blog posts to articulate my beliefs. The blog series (wherein I came up with the term, *UnClobber*) grew into a series of video lectures and eventually formed the foundation for this book.

Who Is *UnClobber* For?

If you feel the church has been wrong to demonize and reject the LGBTQ community but you're still pretty confident the Bible condemns homosexuality, then *UnClobber* is for you.

If you feel drawn to a more inclusive Christian faith but are held back by what you've been taught about the Bible, then *UnClobber* is for you.

If you have close friends or family members who are gay, lesbian, bisexual, transgender, or queer and you love them with your whole heart but your view of the Bible prevents you from fully celebrating them, then *UnClobber* is for you.

If you're already an affirming Christian but are struggling to articulate what you believe about the "Clobber Passages," then *UnClobber* is for you.

If you are LGBT or Q and you grew up in a Christian home or are drawn toward faith in Christ but you have been told—and maybe believe—that God sees you as less-than or despises you or expects you to remain celibate or try and become straight, then *UnClobber* is for you.

If you're a Christian leader who is curious about how a straight, white, formerly conservative evangelical pastor came to an affirming position and now leads a progressive Christian church, then *UnClobber* is for you.

Some of you might be reading this solely for the chapters on the "Clobber Passages." If that is you, read the even-numbered chapters (2, 4, 6, 8, and 10). Others might be more interested in the story of how I came to align my head and my heart on homosexuality and the Bible. If so, read the odd-numbered chapters (1, 3, 5, 7, and 9).

My hope is that some of you might find yourself in my story. Perhaps you can relate when I talk about the season of my life when I believed that homosexuality was a sin but also felt it was the church's job to love and accept the gay community, not condemn and reject them. Or the season of my life when my inner convictions made me feel out of place with those with whom I worked and was in community. Some of you will undoubtedly relate to the loss and rejection I endured as a result of my coming out as an ally for the LGBTQ community. Others may not find themselves in my story in particular, but through reading *UnClobber*, you discover that the Bible you have held dear for so long has been leveraged to condemn an entire segment of the population based on the misuse of half a dozen poorly translated and poorly understood Bible verses. More than all of that, though, I want you to receive hope that your life holds the potential for abundant life when you travel the often-frightening but always-liberating path toward becoming on the outside who you are on the inside.

So walk with me, would you? As I go from a poster boy of conservative evangelicalism, to a conflicted theologian, to an open and affirming Christian, to a fired pastor, to a lost and searching spiritual sojourner, and finally to a co-conspirator for a faith community where the unimaginable comes to life.

I'll begin with the prayer that I say before every sermon I preach,

> Lord, if there is anything I'm about to say that is good, true, or helpful for those on their journey of faith, I pray that it sticks in our minds and clings to our hearts. But if there is anything I'm about to say that is untrue or would be unhelpful for any in their journey, may your grace allow us to forget it the moment we hear it. Amen.

PROLOGUE

———————————→

Summer of 2005
Portland, Oregon

After months of preparation, my vocational identity hinged on the answer to one more question. I glanced at my wife, relieved that I had made it this far. But I knew what was still to come, as though they had saved the juiciest for last.

Kate and I left our new baby at home to make the seventy mile drive north to the district headquarters. This was where young prospects like me came to be interviewed by a panel of seasoned ministers. It was the final step to become a licensed minister in my denomination. Already the interview had lasted more than three hours, which was two hours longer than I was told it typically took.

The room was small, but its high ceilings gave it importance. The decor was noticeably dated, yet it felt warm and familiar. The contrasting floral patterns on virtually every surface reminded me of visiting my grandmother when I was young. As I turned back to the panel of four ministers, I wondered if any of them had perhaps been interviewed in this same room decades ago, back when the furnishings would have been considered new and trendy. They had all been kind and gracious to Kate and me, doling out their questions about the denomination's views on Christology, soteriology, eschatology, and every other -ology imaginable.

For the past five years, I had been working toward, and dreaming of, this moment, when at last I could be called "Pastor." Not that I wanted anyone to actually call me "Pastor Colby." That wasn't it. I felt the formality of such a name ought to be reserved for those with more years under their belts. But oh, how I longed to receive affirmation from an institution that deemed me fit to be a pastor within their organization.

As I sat there, waiting for their final line of questioning, I was anxious that my recently shaken faith might have doomed this interview from the get-go. Had I sat on that rose-colored, rose-patterned loveseat six months prior, at the height of my evangelical training, I'm confident I would have sailed through in thirty minutes, reciting each doctrinal nuance with ease and conviction. It was possible that even to the panel, in that moment, I appeared as a poster boy for the millennial pastor. But a few of my answers to their questionnaire, filled out prior to the interview, raised some red flags. Maybe I wasn't what I appeared.

So they pressed in. And I gave honest responses that eased the uncertainty for their first two flags. Ruth, the eldest minister, with her disarming smile, flipped a few pages and looked my way. Here came the third.

"Colby," she said, "why don't you explain for us your response to question 37 on page 4."

I didn't need to turn there. I knew what she meant.

CHAPTER 1

———————————→

WHEN THE HEAD
AND THE HEART
CAN'T GET ALONG

Carol and Iced Tea

As all good stories do, mine begins in a lesbian's hot tub.

Carol was short, fit, and sported a high and tight haircut. No matter when I saw her, she was dressed in shorts, a polo shirt, and white sneakers. Carol lived across the street from me growing up, and I knew two facts about her: she was a lesbian, and she owned the block's only hot tub.

I was probably eight or nine years old when my mom told me and my two brothers that our neighbor was gay. My mom knew this because Carol had been her PE teacher back in high school, and though I couldn't have appreciated how unusual it was at the time, Carol lived out of the closet in our small town of Albany, Oregon, since as long as my mom could remember.

And I knew she had a hot tub because I could see it through the fence on my route when I delivered newspapers around the neighborhood. Carol subscribed to

1

the *Democrat Herald*, so I interacted with her from time to time as I tossed a paper on her porch or collected her monthly payment.

Even though I was raised in a conservative Baptist home, with a dad who descended from a long line of Baptists, I think it was because my mom was a first-generation Christian that I never got the sense that Carol was anything other than, well, a retired gym teacher who read the paper. You see, while I remember my mom informing the three of us about her former kickball instructor, I don't recall her layering it with negative associations. Sure, Mom taught us that homosexuality was a "sin in the eyes of the Lord," but I think she missed the Sunday school series on homosexuality at First Baptist Church, because she never spoke a word of judgment or condemnation against Carol beyond that. Plus, to the excitement of this particular pre-teen paper boy, she said yes when Carol asked if my brothers and I wanted to swim in her hot tub. I'd never been in a hot tub before, and I wasn't about to let the sinful lifestyle of one of my longtime customers keep me out of the water.

Three things stand out to me about my first time in a hot tub, which also coincided with my first time in the home of someone who wasn't straight. First, the iced tea wasn't very good. I'm pretty sure it was unsweetened Lipton. (No offense, Carol, but this is not the drink of choice for young boys.) Second, her hot tub didn't have any fancy lights, and the jets didn't work. So it amounted to an oversized bath for me and my brothers, a bit of a letdown for my first time. It took me years to buy into the allure of a Jacuzzi. Finally, thinking back on that afternoon, what stands out the most about Carol-the-lesbian and her backyard hot tub was how, well, *normal* she was. She might have been a sinner, but she sure was a nice sinner.

Seeds were planted in my heart that afternoon in the piping hot (if sadly motionless) waters of Carol's tub. I wouldn't come to appreciate that moment until years later, nor would I be aware of the seeds' presence in my heart.

But in the pages that follow I want to tell you the story of how I discovered that both following the beliefs of my head and trusting the convictions of my heart do not have to be mutually exclusive endeavors.

In fact, I believe that the spiritual journey might very well involve the process of aligning these two realities.

Meeting Jesus on Huntington Beach

The summer of '99, before I started my final year of high school, the trajectory of my life changed forever.

I grew up going to church religiously. My mom dragged us every Sunday, both before and after my parents divorced when I was ten years old. Like many kids, I was indifferent on my best days and indignant on my worst. So I surprised even myself when, at seventeen years old, I said yes to Jeremy, who asked if I wanted to go with him to Southern California for a week-long Christian conference called SEMP. I'm sure I agreed to go only because I thought Jeremy, one of my youth pastors, was cool. And I felt special for being invited. Plus, for this Oregon born-and-raised kid, SoCal (Southern California for the uninitiated) was a place of magic and mystique.

SEMP—Students Equipped to Minister to Peers— was an annual conference aimed at training high schoolers in the ways of evangelism. The mornings were spent in classrooms, learning tools such as the Jesus Juke[1] and the Romans Road[2]. In the afternoons, they paired us up two-by-two and sent us out to places like Huntington Beach for random street witnessing.

That first day on the beach, harassing vacationers about the eternal destination of their souls left me feeling like a fraud. It revealed my allegiance to Christianity as being in name only. I felt exposed, like the unsuspecting kid who wore all white to the laser tag birthday party. When I returned to the room I was staying in, I collapsed on the bed and sobbed for a solid twenty minutes.

Sometimes life gives you the gift of standing outside yourself, if only for a moment, to grasp the entirety of the fork splitting your road; a moment when you realize that whichever path you take, whatever you decide in this precise moment, will have consequences for years and years to come. As a teenager, obsessed with being popular and neurotic about standing out, the options before me were this: either proceed as usual and continue to live life for the sole purpose of acquiring attention and affection for myself, or make a dramatic about face (what the biblical writers call "repenting") and devote my energies to bringing attention and affection toward Jesus.

As I lay there in a pool of snot, my pillow soaked with tears, I was confronted with the reality that I had spent the afternoon trying to convince others to follow someone whom I, myself, had never bothered to walk behind. I was introducing strangers to someone I didn't even know. And the separation between who I was on the inside and what I was doing on the outside was suffocating my soul.

I tracked down Jeremy later that night and asked him to pray with me, to help me take that first step down the path, the path where my life would first and foremost be about Jesus. In that moment, I knew the vision I wanted for my life. Like when you plan a long road trip and you may not know every single place you'll stop, but you know the destination and can chart out the general course, I sensed a call on my life then as strong as I still do today: I wanted to be a pastor.

I wanted to give my life to telling people about Jesus. I wanted to study the Bible, teach it, and inspire people to trust God with their lives. I wanted to invite people to consider that the Way of Jesus is the best way for a life of peace, hope, justice, and love. I wanted to shepherd people through the ongoing transformation of love in their lives.

Being a pastor has been a harder journey than I could have imagined that night, when I prayed with Jeremy. I'm not sure I would have taken that path had I known some of the heartbreak awaiting me in full-time ministry. But after being in the game for seventeen years now, I can honestly say I am still chasing after the same vision for my life. And while I may no longer tell random strangers that they are destined for eternal damnation if they don't repeat a magic prayer, my resolve to study the Scriptures, follow Jesus, and invite others to do the same has remained unmoved.

Oversaved

When we got back from SEMP, I was a different person. Whether it was because of my encounter with Jesus for the first time or because of my encounter with Krispy Kreme for the first time, the jury is still out. But there's no question everything changed. I was (as we called it back then) "on fire for the Lord." I began organizing prayer groups, teaching Bible studies, and putting on massive evangelistic events to save all my friends. I was unashamedly passionate about Jesus.

Allow me to pause for a moment and apologize to anyone who knew me between 1999 and 2004. Those years, while my intentions were positive and my heart was in the right place, I was a classic case of being *oversaved*.[3] It was annoying. I know. Every conversation had to be about my faith. Every interaction led to a discussion in theology. No one was safe, not the person next to me on an airplane or the couple at the adjacent table in Starbucks. Most of my childhood friends began to tire of my relentless pursuit to proselytize them. I was a Jesus Freak through and through, and any ridicule I received I wore as a badge of honor, assuming it was the persecution Paul spoke of in the New Testament.

After high school, I abandoned my plans to study graphic design in New York and instead enrolled in a small Christian college in Salem, Oregon, where, to my delight, being a Jesus Freak was a virtue. Rather than being ignored and ostracized, I was sought after and elevated. Being oversaved had become an asset.

Now, I mention all this so that you get a sense for how entrenched I was in conservative evangelical Christianity. I could recite Scripture, defend the creeds, and wax eloquent on the advantages of premillennial dispensationalism with the best of them. And yet, when it came to theology around sexuality, I don't recall spending any time or energy on it. At that time I didn't have any gay friends or family members that I knew of. Carol, a distant memory and merely an acquaintance, remained my sole interaction with someone who was gay. If the topic of homosexuality did come up, whether at school or at church, the conversation served only to reinforce the party line: homosexuality is a sin. It was as much in question as it was to be a liar, a murderer, or an adulterer. And the Bible was seen as unambiguous in its views. Whether or not homosexuality is wrong in the eyes of God was a nonstarter. As a result, I never started.

Which is why it was so surprising to me, as I sat in that high-ceilinged room being interviewed by Ruth and the other three ministers, that I almost didn't get licensed to be a pastor because I had conflicted feelings about LGBTQ people and the church.

No Membership Allowed

"You wrote here," Ruth went on, pointing to my written answers, "that while you agree with the denomination on the issue of homosexuality, you struggle with our church's policies. Can you elaborate on that for us?"

I thought back to the moment that led me to write down that answer. I was walking through our church lobby while reading the policies and procedures manual, squeezing in some study time during my lunch break. I was reading the sections that covered how the church elected their elders, how they allotted vacation time for staff, and what the process was for becoming a church member. And then I read a sentence that unlocked feelings I didn't even know I had.

Essentially it said, "Practicing homosexuals shall not be permitted to become members of the church."

I froze, in the middle of the lobby, unsure of how to decipher my emotions. There was something so jarring about the phrase, "shall not be permitted to become members." It felt like the first time I learned that Augusta National Golf Club, one of our country's most prized golf clubs and host of the annual Masters Tournament, didn't allow African Americans to be members until 1990 and didn't allow women to be members until 2012.

Here was a Christian church, through which I was seeking to become a pastor, that would deny membership to someone because . . . because what, exactly? Because they were attracted to people of the same sex? Or because they had sex with people of the same gender? I wondered what all it took for a person to be considered a "practicing homosexual." Then I saw there was more. It went on to explain that not only could practicing homosexuals not become members but also could not serve in a number of volunteer positions either.

"So let me get this straight," I said to myself, oblivious to the fantastic pun, "the denomination will allow gay people to attend their churches, worship on Sundays, volunteer in a limited capacity—such as where people can't see them or they don't have any leadership—and accept their tithes and offerings without hesitation, but if a gay person seeks membership or wants to use leadership gifts to serve the body, then nothing but rejection awaits?"

At the time, I didn't have proper language to name what was going on for me. But ten years later, with a solid decade of hindsight in my toolbox, I discovered the cause of my unsettled spirit walking through the lobby that day.

Pursuing Integrity

I met with Derek once a week for nine months during 2014. He was my spiritual director, helping me discern the calling and mission of my life. At that point I had gone through multiple painful experiences with churches, and I wondered if perhaps my seventeen-year-old self had been wrong. Distraught and a little freaked out, I turned to Derek to find clarity on who I was and what I should be doing.

During our time together, he had me go through an exercise of mapping out a timeline of my life. Using a large poster board, I wrote on dozens of colored sticky notes to chronicle the significant events and people that had impacted me. It was a brutiful[4] tapestry of my first thirty-two years. One morning, after some intense emotional work, Derek surveyed my timeline while he stroked the stubble on his chin. Right about the point where my tolerance for awkward silence was maxed, he leaned back in the booth at our favorite coffee shop and said, "It seems to me that integrity is important in your life."

"Sure, I guess," I replied, unimpressed with his assessment. "I mean yeah, it's important for me to live upright even when no one is watching." I wondered what his point was. Isn't integrity important to everyone?

"I don't mean that kind of integrity," he continued, "I mean *integrity* in the sense of being integrated—being whole and complete." He gestured to a number of sticky notes on my timeline, "Over and over in your life you have these significant moments that are centered on you not being integrated, where your internal convictions and your external actions are not in alignment."

"Where your internal convictions and your external actions are not in alignment," I repeated in my head, his words exploding like fireworks.

Do you remember the scene in *Fight Club* when Edward Norton finally realizes that he is Tyler Durden? You stare at the screen as the disparate strands of the film all click in to place, the plot suddenly making sense, and you wonder how you could have missed it.

Derek's words that morning were like that. This concept of *integrity*—aligning my external actions with my internal convictions—brought an instantaneous and pro-found clarity to my timeline—to my *life*. As though an optometrist had been giving me only options one and two for thirty-two years, and now, at last, she moved it to three, and everything immediately came into focus.

This movement toward integrity has been my life's aim. Many times unconsciously. Every significant moment in my timeline, and so many of the significant people as well, were all instances of course correction. My traumatic experience as a fraudulent evangelist on Huntington Beach was a perfect example. Derek was right, my soul suffers and my life limps along when I act in ways that are incongruent with my convictions. If I can't genuinely live into what I believe to be true, or if I'm forced to keep parts of myself hidden, or if I have to act one way even though my heart believes another, then basic fruits of the Spirit, such as joy, peace, and goodness, feel unreachable.

Aligning the Head and the Heart

One crucial step toward being integrated, where our internal convictions are aligned with our external realities, is to pay attention when it feels like our head and our heart are in conflict with each other, when what we believe to be true and what we feel to be right are not lining up.

When I look back at that moment in the lobby of my church, reading about the exclusion of "practicing homosexuals," I can now name what was happening in me. My head and my heart were out of alignment. My head was still theologically grounded in conservative evangelicalism—a world in which being gay is unquestionably a sin. Yet my heart was pushing back with a sense of injustice when I read how my church lived out that theology.

Homosexuality might be wrong, I reasoned, but no more wrong than excluding people—real human beings—from being members in a church or using their God-given gifts, right?

Not long after this jarring moment of realization, I had to finish the questionnaire for my licensing process. There were no questions about sexuality, but toward the end there was a blank space with the words "Any other thoughts you'd like to share with us?" I didn't have to, of course, but I wrote about how I agreed with the denomination about the sinfulness of homosexuality but struggled with the policies on membership and volunteerism.

And *that* was the line on page 4, question 37, that Ruth asked me about so many years ago.

I can't recall exactly how I responded, but whatever I said must have assuaged their anxiety because they ended up granting me licensure. And so the summer of 2005 stands out for two reasons: one, I had finally become a pastor; and two, it was the first time I was conscious of the tension between my head and my heart on the issue of the Bible and homosexuality.

Over the past several years, while working alongside and ministering to the LGBTQ community and straight allies alike, I've learned that this tension is not uncommon. Many people find themselves with this sort of posture. A place you could call "open" but not "affirming." They might feel that the church has mistreated those who identify as gay, lesbian, bisexual, or transgender, and so they want to live with open arms and open hearts, but they can't go all the way to affirmation because of their conviction that the Bible condemns such "lifestyles." This tension between the head and the heart can be found in all but the most fundamental tribes of Christianity. To be sure, many good, loving, kind, and gracious Christians would never join a Westboro Baptist picket line, and yet marching in their hometown's Pride Parade is just as far-fetched. For those with loved ones who identify as LGBTQ, this head-heart tension is amplified by deep mourning. Many are desperate for a way to harmonize their love for friends or family members with their commitment to an honest and accurate understanding of the Bible.

As for me, leaving the district headquarters that day, freshly minted as a pastor, I was unaware that I had begun a journey toward alignment on the subject of homosexuality, a journey that would take about five years. Yet that was only the beginning. As it turns out, finding alignment on the Bible and homosexuality would launch me in to yet another journey of finding alignment between my internal convictions and my external actions as a pastor in full-time ministry.

Moving to the Desert

One year after getting licensed, Kate and I left the rain for the sun. We picked up and moved from Salem, Oregon, to Chandler, Arizona, a burgeoning suburb of southeast Phoenix. I had just been hired to be the Pastor of Worship and Arts at a young church plant of about five years. Full of loving and generous people, it was an ideal place for me to grow as a worship pastor. They granted me the freedom to explore creative ways to engage people in corporate worship and empower artists to make art. During my five years there, the church grew from two hundred to fifteen hundred, and we assisted in the transformation of hundreds of people's lives.

And yet . . .

Kate and I couldn't have anticipated where our spiritual journeys with Christ would take us. Nor did we realize how conservative our new environment would be. You see, not long after getting licensed (by the skin of my teeth), I picked up a copy of Brian McLaren's *A New Kind of Christian*. I had read an interview with Rob Bell where he mentioned Brian's book as one that made a significant impact on him.

I would feel that same impact.

Reading *A New Kind of Christian* was an eye-opening experience. For the first time, I discovered that there exists other expressions and understandings of Christianity than the Western/Protestant/Evangelical/Baptist version I had consumed hook, line, and sinker in church and college. Through Brian, I learned it was okay to ask questions, and it was okay to not know all the answers. This was simultaneously terrifying and liberating for me, as I had always prided myself on being the Bible Answer Man, the guy people could come to with questions about God, the Bible, and faith. I would impress them with my wisdom at such a young age, always giving an answer to their questions — even if I had to make one up to sound smart.

After I finished McLaren's book, I found myself on a course that would open my mind to all sorts of beautiful realities about the religion I adhered to, the God I worshiped, and the Lord I followed. But this new journey, while taking me deeper into the heart of God's dream for creation and closer to the core of Jesus' kingdom message, also put increasing distance between me and the conservative theology I grew up with. As a result, after a few years in Arizona it became painfully obvious that we might not be as great a fit at our new church as we would have hoped.

My journey away from conservative evangelicalism was met with fear and frustration from others in our church. I discovered that many evangelicals hold their beliefs with such clenched fists that they fear and violently resist any questions or challenges to their convictions. Being in that culture, Kate and I learned to keep most of the changes that were happening in our hearts to ourselves because we didn't feel safe voicing our questions or talking about our doubts. And the few times we did open up felt like trying to feed peas to a toddler: it's messy, confusing, and nobody feels good afterward.

We had been there just over a year when it was presidential election season, Obama vs. McCain. Neither Kate nor I knew who we would vote for yet, seeing as how we were in the midst of so much theological and ideological transition, but when people from our church forwarded a mass email about an outlandish story involving Barack Obama, it seemed prudent to investigate its veracity. As it turns out, the truth was a simple Snopes search away. However, when we replied to everyone with the link that revealed how the original story was fabricated, we inadvertently set off a storm of "concern"[5] in the church community about the "liberal" pastor and his wife. One lady was concerned enough to show up at our house the following night and warn us, "If you vote for Obama, then the blood of unborn babies will be on your hands."

I shared a YouTube video one day on Facebook about a tighter gun policy that had passed in New York City. The next week a friend of mine told me over lunch, "I could not bring myself to worship with you on Sunday because I kept thinking about that video you posted and how you're against guns."

Then there was the John Piper video I shared online, in which he suggests that wives should endure abuse from their husbands, and I called it a #pastorFAIL, only to be told by people in my church that I shouldn't criticize John Piper. There was also the time at an elder board meeting where I spoke up on behalf of a friend of mine—a recently discharged elder whose marriage was falling apart—because the board was suggesting that if he tried to attend church, then they would walk him back out the front door. To which I responded, "Then I guess I'll take him around to the back door."

In short, while I think most everyone at the church loved me, and really liked what I brought to the worship and arts ministries, I wasn't fitting the mold of what a Christian pastor should look like. The more I grew into my newfound convictions, the more my ideas and questions were a threat to established theological systems. I believe, over time, they came to view me as the "liberal-hippie-peace-loving pastor who questioned the faith and was easy on sin!"

Meh, I suppose they weren't too far off.

The Power of Pizza and a Movie

Miraculously, we had procured a babysitter for the evening, affording us the opportunity to enjoy a night out at a new pizza place. As we waited for our food to arrive, conscious of the silence that eerily fills the space when your kids aren't around, Kate and I attempted a feat couples with young children rarely enjoy: a conversation.

"So what do you think about homosexuality?" I asked Kate, fidgeting with my napkin.

It was a Friday night in mid-September 2010. We'd been in Arizona for four years, and each passing year brought more and more distance between our theology and that of the church. I can't recall why the topic of homosexuality came up that night, but it had been a while since either of us had talked about it.

I listened as Kate explained that she no longer believed that being gay was a sin. She had moved to a new place in her life, that of a fully inclusive Christian, open and affirming of the LGBTQ community. It was amazing how far we had come, both together and as individuals. The journey would have been a whole lot scarier and harder had one of us traveled it alone.

Even as I enjoyed my thin crust margherita pizza, listening to Kate share her newfound resolution, I was still unconvinced with regard to the Bible. During my time in Arizona, I deconstructed most of the faith I was raised with and established during college. While I was steadily reconstructing some aspects of my theology, I still had not spent time exploring the Clobber Passages. The tension between my head and my heart remained. And while I may have felt less confident that the Bible condemned homosexuality, I still didn't have peace on the issue. I recall telling Kate that night, "While I'm no longer prepared to call gay people sinful or judge them, I still think that it's not God's best intention for humanity."

We left that night with a commitment to keep the conversation going. So a couple weeks later when we heard about a documentary called "For the Bible Tells Me So," which shares the stories of five families who navigate having a child who identifies as gay or lesbian, we sat down to watch it together. The movie explores the relationship between religion and homosexuality. It unpacks the history of how the Religious Right has stigmatized and oppressed the LGBTQ community. What impacted me the most, however, were the powerful stories of men and women who followed after God and sought an honest relationship with Christ but who were also attracted to members of the same sex. Their stories normalized the issue for me. In fact, after watching that movie, I realized that this isn't an issue. That's a horrible word to use. This is about real people with real stories.

The film also provided what I was longing for: resources for an honest exploration of the Clobber Passages that offered alternative understandings and interpretations. The next few weeks involved a flurry of blog reading as I discovered for the first time that genuine followers of Jesus had studied this material and come to different conclusions on the issue . . . er, I mean, about the people who identify as LGBTQ.

I read scholars who explained that the destruction of Sodom and Gomorrah had nothing to do with homosexuality. I learned that the meaning of the word *abomination* in Leviticus is a far cry from describing behavior that is inherently sinful. I was exposed to careful readings of Paul's letters, in which I had always believed he spoke with such clarity. But fresh insights revealed that perhaps we've gotten him wrong. The time I spent poring over the Clobber Passages were laying the foundation for what would eventually become this book.

Slowly, the theological corners of my brain let in light and I could see how we, how *I*, had misused the Bible on homosexuality. My heart traveled deeper into the lush fields of compassion and mercy and turned to watch as my mind at long last allowed the warmth of the sun and the promise of integrity to coax it out of its cave.

The aligning had begun.

Apologizing on the Polar Express

I thought my days of interrupting strangers in order to talk about Jesus were behind me, but it was mid-December when an interaction with a couple on a train solidified for me that the alignment between my head and my heart was complete.

Our friends Justin and Meghan invited us to join their family on a Polar Express experience up in northern Arizona. Every Christmastime, an old train and its station get converted to resemble the North Pole. Families, dressed in their pajamas, board a gorgeous steam engine to drink hot cocoa and visit Santa, who gives each kid a jingling bell.

On the train we sat next to a family of two dads with their adorable four-year-old girl in Snow White jammies, who assumed that everyone around her was her best friend. She wasn't wrong. I watched as her dads doted on her every move, lighting up the cabin with their joy. With kindness and patience, they redirected her from jumping on too many people's laps, but some people (like me) didn't mind the intrusion. It was obvious that their daughter's excitement to meet Santa matched—if not surpassed—that of our own boys, and her dads' anticipation for their child to see Santa was equal to Kate's and mine.

In other words, they were a normal family.

When the trip to the North Pole and Santa's Shop concluded, the train returned to the station with cabins full of bell-ringing, cocoa-loaded children. As we gathered our belongings and prepared to disembark, I found myself turning to face the dads of the young girl, compelled by something, but I wasn't sure what.

"Excuse me," I said, for some odd reason, "but I'm a pastor, and I wonder if I might have a moment of your time?"

They exchanged glances with one another, bracing themselves for what might come next. Undeterred—even if I should have been—I pressed on.

"I would like to apologize on behalf of the Christian church," I stated, as though I had such authority, "for the ways in which our judgmental and narrow-minded posture has made the LGBTQ community feel like second-class people. I'm sorry for how we have told you that you are damaged or broken in ways that straight people never have to deal with, and how we demand that you have to change who you are if you want to be right with God. I'm sorry for the hate, the fear, and the intolerance."

They, smiled, nodded, and said thanks. Then they explained that they are part of a loving church community who had always welcomed and accepted them. So while they hadn't experienced the things I had apologized for, they said I was sweet for saying so nonetheless.

I exited the train and realized that the unprovoked apology I pitched to those gentlemen was not for them.

It was for me.

The Hero's Journey

The journey of the hero in ancient mythology is a perfect illustration for the spiritual journey. There are four stages: First there is the summons, followed by a series of obstacles, after which comes the receiving of a gift, and finally the return to community to live it out. Alexander J. Shaia refers to this as the universal fourfold pattern of life and transformation.[6] I'm no hero, but I can see how my journey in this particular area followed this progression.

It began with a call, as I awakened to the mistreatment and alienation of the LGBTQ community within the church, through disallowing them membership and rejecting their ability to serve.

With the tension between my head and my heart established, and feeling like I'd stumbled into the summons, I then faced a series of challenges, both external (such as almost not getting licensed to be a pastor) and internal (asking challenging questions about whether or not I'd understood the Scriptures correctly). Reading different perspectives on the Clobber Passages and listening to the stories of those who wrestled with being both gay and Christian helped me work through the obstacles.

The reward for overcoming these challenges was to receive the gift, the joy, of an integrated self. My head and my heart were at last in alignment. For the first time, I could see how the Scriptures did not condemn people who were born with same-sex attraction, nor did it condemn loving, committed, mutually honoring, and respecting relationships between people of the same sex.

Yet that is not the final stage in the hero's journey. She must return to where she came from and learn how to live in community once again as a new version of herself. She must refuse to be pulled back to who she was prior to her journey but also not be content to forsake her community.

As Thelma told Louise, "Something has crossed over in me, and I can't go back."[7]

Something indeed had crossed over in me. Yet I was still a pastor in a large, conservative, evangelical church. Was there a way to return to the community and integrate my newly aligned self? Could I find alignment between my new internal convictions and my established external reality?

What started in Carol-the-lesbian's hot tub was only the beginning.

But for the record, I still don't like unsweetened Lipton iced tea.

CHAPTER 2

---→

RETHINKING OUR MISUSE OF THE BIBLE

Twisting Scripture

Have you ever misused the Bible?

Before you answer that, I'll share two examples of how I have: first with Jenny, then with Dennis. Maybe then you will have the courage to answer honestly.

I dated Jenny for about three months in high school. She was a senior, and I was a sophomore, which, looking back, was probably the main reason for my participation in the relationship. Well, that, and the fact that my older brother had the hots for her. I like to win—what can I say?

But after a few months, when the initial awesomeness of dating a senior wore off, I was ready to move on. Unsure of how to navigate such treacherous territory—and a solid fifteen years before either Adele or Taylor Swift could lead the way—I wanted to find a way to break up that would appear both noble and kind. I didn't want to hurt her feelings; she was a great girl. Then it occurred to me: I was a Christian, and she was not.

Perfect.

So one night I explained to her that the Bible says, "Do not be unequally yoked with unbelievers."[1] Therefore, I had no choice. "As wonderful as you are, Jenny," I sighed, "I must follow the words of God in the Bible."

If she never showed much interest in Christianity *before* that moment, I'm confident I didn't help the cause.

As for Dennis, he and I were attached at the hip for about two years at the end of high school and the beginning of college. We played in a band together, we were both interns at church, and we were convinced that our friendship made the world a better (or at least funnier) place. Before Dennis and I became friends, he ran with the stoner crowd at school. Then he found Jesus around the same time I did, and together our oversaved selves focused our energies and passions on leading worship and evangelizing the world.

One night, Dennis confessed to me that he had backslidden.[2] The lure of smoking pot and drinking beer had overcome him. I was devastated. In my mind at that time, my best friend, my partner in crime, had stumbled mightily. Over the next year or so, he would bounce back and forth between "being right with the Lord" and "falling back in to sin," as we called it back then.

One morning, while diligently doing my daily devotions, I came across 1 Corinthians 5:11, "But now I'm writing to you not to associate with anyone who calls themselves 'brother' or 'sister' who is sexually immoral, greedy, someone who worships false gods, an abusive person, a drunk, or a swindler. Don't even eat with anyone like this." It hit me like a Mack truck: I can't hang out with Dennis any more. I was convinced that Dennis was the backslidden brother Paul was describing.

So that night I sat him down in my bedroom, read the verse out loud, and from high atop my horse explained that I had to stop hanging out with him. "I love you, man, but Paul says that I shouldn't even eat with you. No more late night runs to ABC Chinese for Szechuan chicken. No more devouring a dozen maple bars in one sitting. And definitely no more playing in a Christian soft rock band together."[3]

And that was it. I cut off my best friend just like that. Sure it was painful, but what choice did I have? If I was going to take the Bible seriously and not cherry-pick the verses that suited me, then I needed to heed the words of Paul and disassociate myself from Dennis.

Five years later, when I had long since realized how absurd I had been, I was fortunate enough to catch up with Dennis one evening and humbly ask for his forgiveness. Always the more compassionate one, he gave it without hesitation. But there was no going back. We had drifted much too far apart. The damage had been done.

All because I had misused the Bible.

Living Out Bad Interpretations

Those two stories illustrate two ways in which I think people can misuse the Bible. The first, as with Jenny, is more devious and manipulative. It happens when we twist the Bible to defend our behavior. Deep inside I knew the verse wasn't about high school dating relationships, but I misused it to get what I wanted. Think of the husband who distorts Paul's words about marriage in order to force his wife to go to bed with him, or the pastors who twist Scripture to guilt their congregations into tithing more money.

Those are gross misuses of the Bible, to be sure, but this book is about another type of misuse, one that stems more from a misunderstanding or a bad interpretation than from outright manipulation. This type of misuse, as illustrated in my relationship with Dennis, is categorically different. We can be convinced that the Bible teaches XYZ, and so, in our effort to live biblically, we adjust our lives—not because we are coldhearted, or because we are ignoring Scripture, but because as best as we can tell (or, as is often the case, have been told by others) the Bible demands it of us.

When it comes to homosexuality and the Bible, this is the most prevalent posture I have come across. Where good-hearted Christians, who are doing their best to line their lives up with Scripture, are convinced that the Bible condemns homosexuality and same-sex relationships. So even though they may want to support or remain in relationship with their gay friends, they are choosing instead to honor their understanding of the Bible. But I believe such an understanding of the Bible is a result of bad interpretations of the Clobber Passages, causing people to recklessly assume an anti-gay posture. This then leads to behavior from Christians, the church, and society (since society for so long has taken its cues from the Judeo-Christian perspective) that is appalling and shameful, not to mention hurtful and damaging.

When my friends Rebecca and Valerie, with their nine-month-old daughter Ella, are told that family members won't be coming to Thanksgiving because of their "sinful lifestyle," I think we're misusing the Bible.

When a judge in Utah rules that a foster child be removed from a married same-sex couple and placed in a home with a mom and dad, because he believes it's better for the emotional stability of the child, I think we're misusing the Bible.

When LGBTQ youth are four times more likely to attempt suicide than their straight peers and then eight times more likely to attempt suicide when they live in a home with a family that rejects them,[4] I think we're misusing the Bible.

When churches come out as fully welcoming and affirming and as a result are kicked out of their denominations, or watch as half their people leave, I think we're misusing the Bible.

I'm writing this book because when you know better, you do better. And I think the six passages in the Bible that have traditionally been used to reject an entire subset of our population have not been interpreted well, and therefore, have not been used well.

I think it is time we rethink our misuse of the Bible on homosexuality.

Going on a Bear Hunt

One of my favorite books, which I've read to all four of our boys growing up, is *We're Going on a Bear Hunt.* In it, the bear-hunting party faces a series of natural obstacles threatening to throw their beautiful day off course. At each turn, whether it's a deep, cold river or thick, oozy mud, they must face the hard truth: they can't go over it, and they can't go under it . . . no, they must go through it.

And so it is with the Clobber Passages. While there might be a temptation by some, in an effort to unchain the Bible from an anti-gay perspective, to simply dismiss the Bible as not being authoritative or to toss out verses for one reason or another, I am not compelled by such arguments.

I am an orthodox Christian who follows the Way of Jesus and who believes in his death and resurrection. I love the Holy Scriptures and find in them a revealing of who God is and a record of how God has uniquely interacted with humanity throughout the history of the Jewish people. I stand behind, and love, Paul's words to Timothy, "Every scripture is inspired by God and is useful for teaching, for showing mistakes, for correcting, and for training character, so that the person who belongs to God can be equipped to do everything that is good" (2 Tim. 3:16–17). My view of Scripture is, I'm sure, high by some standards and low by others, but when it comes down to it, I want to study it, seek to understand—and be understood by[5]—it, and critically engage it in ways that honor how and why they were written, who wrote them, and to whom they were addressed. In short, it would be a mistake to dismiss me or write me off as someone who doesn't take the Bible seriously, even if you disagree with my conclusions.

With each of the UnClobbering chapters in this book I will demonstrate how the passages in question have been either mistranslated, misunderstood, or both, and how that has led to a misuse of the Bible. A misuse that has resulted in the marginalization and demonization of men and women who were not born with attractions for only the opposite sex.

In Genesis, for instance, the Bible has been misused to blame gay people for natural disasters. Why? Because we've been led to believe that the sin of Sodom and Gomorrah was homosexuality. Since God destroyed cities once before because of such wickedness, it stands to reason that perhaps God would do it again. But does the Bible indeed identify homosexuality as the sin of Sodom or Gomorrah?

In Leviticus, the Bible has been misused to label the LGBTQ community as abominations, as people who are less-than-human. Why? Because two verses in the Priestly Code refer to a type of sexual activity between two men as "an abomination." But what did that mean then? And does it still mean that today?

In perhaps the most well-known Clobber passage, Paul talks of same-sex activity in the context of people who have turned their backs on God and describes how divine wrath is heaped on them (Rom. 1). Misusing that passage has led people to deny that someone can be both gay and Christian. But what if we've misunderstood what Paul was doing in this passage?

Finally, Paul, in two letters (one to Corinth, another to his friend, Timothy), lists two activities as precluding a person from being participants in the Kingdom of God. English Bibles translate Paul as saying, "homosexuality" or "practicing homosexuals," which has resulted in people misusing these verses to exclude LGBTQ people from the church. But was that what Paul had in mind?

By looking at the historical context, the context of the passage in question, and other interpretive tools, I hope to help you discover that there is good reason to call into question how the church has historically handled the Clobber Passages. Even more so, there are good reasons to walk away from these verses with a renewed appreciation for the Bible and the biblical authors and to be an open and affirming Christian who also believes in the inspiration and authority of the Scriptures.

It's Not about Being Right

Even though it has served me well at times in life, I would say that one of my biggest weaknesses is my incessant need to be right. As my wife can attest, I will go out of my way to find some creative or clever defense to explain why it is that you might *perceive* me to be wrong, but in fact, as the data I'm about to present you shows, I am correct. As I said in the last chapter, this showed up in my cherished identity as the go-to Bible Answer Man. Knowing the answer and being right are like carbs and sugar — I crave them and they give me momentary jolts of energy, but obsessing over them will lead only to unhealthiness.

I tell you this because it's important to say from the beginning that I do not claim to have the right interpretation of the Clobber Passages, as much as I may wish I do or want you to think that I do. And if anyone tells you that *they* have the right interpretation, you should be suspicious. In these six passages, we are dealing with cultures and languages thousands of years removed from our own, and we are looking for answers to complex questions that, in many ways, are unique to our time in history. This is not to say that any attempt at understanding them is hopeless, but an honest approach should include the presupposition that we should not expect 100 percent certainty. This is also not to say that some interpretations can't be held up as being more reflective of the context, or more likely to be what the authors were getting at, than others.

That is what I will show as we UnClobber the Bible on homosexuality—that there are ways of understanding these six passages, grounded in textual and historical context, that offer alternative understandings of the Bible's view toward homosexuality and same-sex relationships than what the church has historically taught.

The Bible does not condemn those who are born with same-sex attraction, or who are attracted to both sexes, or attracted to neither. The Bible does not condemn those who are born with the biology of one gender but identify as another. The Bible does not condemn any and all sex acts between the same sex. To someone who is lesbian, gay, transgender, bisexual, or queer and who is in a loving, God-honoring, committed relationship, the Bible does not say, "You are not a Christian; you are not saved; you do not belong in the Kingdom of Heaven."

So it's time we stop saying that it does.

It's Going to Take a Lot of Words

Whenever he is caught or questioned about breaking a house rule, one of my sons will launch into a long-winded explanation of what transpired. The longer he talks, the more his mother and I are convinced of his guilt. His myriad words reveal his elaborate attempt to justify his choices.

In a similar way, I often feel that those of us who advocate for a reading of the Bible that does not lead to condemnation of gay people are at a disadvantage. The traditional interpretation of the Clobber Passages is easier to articulate and defend. It has the clarity of English translations and the choir of church history on its side. All they have to do to satisfy their theological demand is open up their Bibles and read in plain words that "those who practice homosexuality will not inherit the kingdom of God" (see 1 Cor. 6:9) or "women exchanged natural relations for unnatural

. . . and men were consumed with passion for one another, committing shameless acts" (see Rom. 1:26–27).

It appears so straightforward and obvious.

And then when people like me offer alternative ways to understand the Clobber Passages, it can come across as trying to find a way to justify it all—like my son. When I type a sentence such as, "But is that *really* what Paul meant?" I hear the voice of the critic dismissing me with, "'That is precisely what the serpent said to Eve in the Garden! *Did God really say . . . ?'*"

But as I see it, it is inevitable—if not necessary—that any attempt to UnClobber the Bible will involve a lot of explanation. Great effort will be required to unpack the Greek, explore the context, and appeal to information and considerations outside the biblical text. And I'm sure that can sound exhausting to those with the traditional perspective, like I am stretching beyond reason or ignoring the "plain meaning of the text."

Recently I read Elizabeth Gilbert's *The Signature of All Things*, a brilliant novel set, in part, in early 1800s America. In one striking scene, Professor Peck lectures some dinner guests about the superiority of white people over Negroes [*sic*]. Prudence, the sister of the protagonist Alma, pushes back against the professor's claims. She dares suggest that blacks and whites are the same species, not different. Professor Peck responds,

> "The *superiority* of the white man should be clear to anyone with the faintest education in human history and origin. . . . The Negro shows an overexpression of emotional senses, which accounts for his infamous absence of self-control. We see this demonstrated in his facial structure. There is altogether too much eye, lip, nose, and ear—which is to say that the Negro cannot help but become overstimulated by his senses. Thus, he is capable of the warmest affection, but also the darkest violence."[6]

Imagine being like Prudence, one of the lone voices to challenge popular assumptions about differences between races. There's no question you would fight an uphill battle as you combat long-held prejudices and deeply entrenched beliefs. You'd be written off by the Professor Pecks of the world as ignoring the plain and obvious truth. It would fall on deaf ears as you plead for people to consider genetics or to consider how society shapes us to think as we do. You'd be accused of distorting what we already know and what we've always known.

Pushing back against long-held beliefs about the Bible and homosexuality (and deeply entrenched prejudices against the gay community) feels like that at times. We fight an uphill battle as we plead with Christians to stay at the table long enough to hear us out. The task isn't easy, and many people do not want to (or are not ready to) hear that maybe we've misused the Bible.

But I think the task is important and much needed. Hence I offer the thousands of words in this book to try and get us to rethink a couple of dozen words from the Bible.

At the end of the day, for Christians who see the Bible as being authoritative in their lives, how they understand the Clobber Passages matters. If the only interpretation they have ever heard convinces them that the Bible, and therefore God, stands in opposition to homosexuality, then that will inform how they live. It will affect how they treat their LGBTQ friends and family.

Poor interpretations lead to misusing the Bible. And real people get hurt as a result.

We've Done It Before

I recognize that for some readers my suggestion that the Bible has been "misused" might sound a bit pompous. Who am I, really, to turn my nose at nearly two thousand years of what could, in all fairness, be described as consensus about how the church has positioned itself toward those among us whose natural inclination is for intimacy with people of the same sex? At some point, you might argue, we need to simply accept that millions of men and women of the faith throughout history can't all have been wrong about, or misused, the Bible, right?

And yet . . .

Isn't that exactly what happened when bold voices dared insist that we misused the Bible in how we see people of color? In how we understand the sun, the earth, and who revolves around what? And (for some people, at least) in how we've treated women? This idea that "the Bible has been misused" is not new by any means, and there is precedent for such a move.

Beyond modern examples, I'm reminded of how the early church was challenged by their own misuse of the Bible when it came to their posture toward Gentiles. Peter, in Acts 10, was gently moved toward this mindfulness through a vision of unclean animals and a visit with Cornelius. Then, in Acts 15, some members of the community demanded, "The Gentiles must be circumcised. They must be required to keep the Law from Moses" (Acts 15:5; referencing Lev. 12:3). Paul and Barnabas argued against this viewpoint, leading to the Jerusalem Council, which resulted in a paradigm-shattering decision on the church's belief and practice toward Gentiles, "The Holy Spirit has led us to the decision that no burden should be placed on you other than these essentials . . . " (Acts 15:28). In short, the first Christian leaders were confronted by the reality that they were misusing the Bible, and a much-needed course correction was put in place.

So when I invite us to consider that we have misused the Bible on homosexuality, not everyone will agree with me, obviously. But my hope, if you *do* disagree with me, is that it's because you fundamentally feel differently about how to interpret the Clobber Passages, and *not* because you think it's absurd, or inappropriate, or that it somehow could not be a Spirit-led endeavor to challenge how the church has historically understood the Bible on a certain issue. The church has been wrong before; let us not be so naive as to think it can't happen again.

I hope you'll join me as we go on a bear hunt and seek to UnClobber the Clobber Passages.

But first, I need to tell you what happened to me in Arizona when I tried to suggest that we have misused the Bible on homosexuality.

CHAPTER 3

———————————→

HOW FACEBOOK GOT
ME FIRED

Six Words

It took Mikhail Gorbachev two words to throw Russian support behind the dismantling of the Berlin Wall: "Why not?"[1]

It took Julius Caesar three words to report his decisive Roman military victory: "*Veni, vidi, vici.*"

It took Marie Antoinette four words to incite the French Revolution: "Let them eat cake."

It took René Descartes five words to lay the foundation for Western philosophy: "I think, therefore I am."

And it took me six words to undo half a decade of ministry with a large church outside Phoenix, Arizona.

Perhaps not on the same scale, I'll grant you that. But I would nonetheless like to tell you the story of how my journey toward alignment involved a Facebook post that eventually got me fired in the fall of 2011.

But first, let's back up to that March, when the first steps of that particular journey began.

Black Sharpies and White Sheets

Three months after my gratuitous apology aboard the Polar Express, I went to the Catalyst West Coast conference in Orange County with the other pastors from our church. Catalyst is an annual conference for church leaders, and that year they set up an interactive arts area in a small chapel on the west side of the campus. We were invited to meditate, reflect, and participate in hands-on creative expressions of worship at our leisure throughout the conference.

Before lunch one afternoon I wandered to the chapel and was drawn toward a display in the back. There were three massive white sheets suspended by poles and wires, forming an eight-foot-tall box with one open side where you could enter. Black sharpies were scattered throughout the display. The idea was to write out a confession anywhere on the sheet, making a large art installation of confessions from around the country. Being a fan of art, sharpies, and interactive worship experiences, I grabbed the nearest marker and stepped in.

Now, just prior to heading over to the chapel, I had listened to an intensely honest keynote presentation by Dr. John Perkins, an extraordinary man who marched in the civil rights movement alongside Martin Luther King Jr. As I crossed the threshold of the sheet-box and looked around me, I noticed how the weight of his words slowed everyone's walk, including my own. We shuffled around, collectively bothered by the harsh reality of his message. A message of how the stain on our nation's history caused by segregation can still be felt. Like a red wine spill on dark carpet, you can wipe it up and believe it's clean, but if you touch it in the right place, you're reminded of its presence. Men and women are still alive, he reminded us, who witnessed firsthand a country once organized around two water fountains, two restaurants, and two buses. He lamented the churches of the past that supported segregation and, prior to that, slavery, in both cases using the Word of God to defend their demoniacal positions.

How many followers of Jesus—I angrily wondered, afraid of the answer—knew it was wrong to discriminate against people based on their skin color, but did nothing about it? How many stayed silent?

Can you imagine what it must be like *now* for those who back *then* were one of the fear-filled silent Christians? Can you fathom being eighty years old and having to live with the reality that, in your heart, you opposed racial segregation, but in your actions you did and said nothing about it?

And what about those who practiced discrimination just because their church or their pastor told them it was the will of God—all because of their radical misuse of a handful of verses? Oh, the regret and shame they must live with, as they look back and realize that they allowed a few sentences from Scripture to trump their capacity for reason, compassion, and love. How heartbreaking it must be, to wake up each day knowing that you stood on the wrong side of history.

All those thoughts were swirling in my mind as I walked to the chapel and entered the confessional. Without planning ahead what I was going to write, I popped off the cap, found a spot high up on the wall with plenty of blank space (a benefit of being almost 6'3"), and let my inner spirit lead:

God, I do not want my future self to be ashamed of my present self. I do not want to remain silent and do nothing about discrimination toward the LGBTQ community. As the world continues changing and we look back on these times 50 years from now and wonder how we could have gotten this issue so wrong, I do not want to have been one of the fear-filled silent ones.

I backed away from the sheet and surveyed the room. Hoping no one from my church was in the chapel . . . but also semi-sorta-kinda secretly wishing they were.

When I reflect on that moment, I can see how, like the seventeen-year-old Colby, who wept on his bed after a day of street-witnessing, this was another liminal moment when I was conscious of a fork in the road. But unlike the soggy pillowcase of '99, as I placed the cap back on my pen and stared at my confession, it occurred to me that simply by writing those words and externalizing my inner convictions, I had already decided which path I'd walk.

Without a doubt, this was the way forward.

The Naaman Effect

Over the next six months, after that pivotal confession at Catalyst, I struggled to keep my chin up at church. The chasm between where I was landing theologically on a number of points and where the church's leadership remained was ever expanding. What I call "The Naaman Effect" was wearing off.

The Naaman Effect comes from an ancient story found in 2 Kings 5.[2] In short, Naaman was commander of the army and the right-hand man of the King of Aram. When he contracted leprosy, he journeyed to Israel to find a great prophet who could cure him. Enter Elisha. Elisha told Naaman to bathe in the Jordan River, and even though Naaman found the treatment plan absurd, he acquiesced. Though he was rewarded with a healed body, what happened next was even more remarkable.

After returning to Elisha, Naaman declared, "Now I know there is no God anywhere on earth except in Israel!" (2 Kgs. 5:15). This is an unbelievable statement, for Naaman was now convinced that the pagan god of his hometown, Rimmon, the god he grew up worshiping and hearing stories about, was a lie. His worldview had been dramatically altered, and he now stood with a new conviction that Yahweh is the One True God.

But this put Naaman in an awkward position. When his entire community worshiped Rimmon, how could he return home and do his job with his newfound belief in the God of Israel? Knowing he would have to participate in worship to a god he knew was not real, he asked this of Elisha, "But may the LORD forgive your servant for this one thing: When my master comes into Rimmon's temple to bow down there and is leaning on my arm, I must also bow down in Rimmon's temple. *When I bow down in Rimmon's temple, may the LORD forgive your servant for doing that*" (2 Kgs. 5:18, emphasis added).

In other words, Naaman asked Elisha if the Lord would be merciful toward him if he didn't fully live out his newfound convictions.

Elisha replied, "You fool, Naaman! The LORD has healed you this day, and yet you intend to commit idolatry? Do not be a coward! You shall not be permitted to live a lie. Return to Aram and declare that you have found the One True God!"

Actually, no he didn't. That's not what Elisha said.

Elisha replied, "Go in *peace*" (v. 19, emphasis added).

He blessed Naaman to return home and *not fully live into his new convictions*. He told Naaman to go, with peace in his heart, and be okay with reintegrating into the community that he no longer agreed with.

So the Naaman Effect is when we receive grace and peace from God to live in a state of misalignment. We own new convictions, yet we keep them to ourselves as we attempt to stay in community with people who think and feel differently. This ancient story offered me respite from much of the tension, helping me get through the final two years at my unaffirming church without feeling like a total fraud.

But there's a catch: I don't think the Naaman Effect is meant to last forever.

I believe God's Spirit will eventually call us to a place beyond the Naaman Effect, to a place of wholeness, integrity, and alignment. For me, that happened in the fall of 2011.

Don't Ask, Don't Tell

In February 1994, the Clinton administration enacted a military ban against open gays and lesbians serving in the military. This meant that service members, if they identified as gay, were not to say so, lest they be kicked out. It also meant that their superiors were not allowed to inquire about their sexuality. For obvious reasons, the law would come to be known as "Don't Ask, Don't Tell" (hereafter referred to as DADT).

I was vaguely aware of the protocol prior to the week I got fired. My limited understanding of DADT boiled down to an issue of discrimination, pure and simple. It seemed inherently un-American to prohibit men and women from serving our country (and even dying for us) if they preferred to cuddle with a person of the same sex.

My lead pastor in Arizona, Jonathan, had a mantra: "There is no room for discrimination in the Kingdom of God." I loved that phrase, as did hundreds of other people. We talked at length about defending the orphan and the widow, speaking out against violence toward women, and bridging the gaps of racial inequality. Discriminating against someone because of their gender, their ethnicity, or their socioeconomic status was not tolerated in our church, just as it isn't in the Kingdom of God.

Yet in my five years there, neither the church at large nor the staff ever discussed the issue of sexuality. It was assumed, I think, that everyone held the traditional, conservative position. No one talked about their beliefs on the Bible and homosexuality, no one talked about their gay friends or family, and no one asked anyone else about their opinions.

Come to think of it, we practiced "don't ask, don't tell."

Which is why, even though I had new convictions on the matter, no one else in the church knew. I could have guessed, however, that my opinion would be not only in the minority in the church but also unwelcome and threatening to many.

I'm Glad This Day Finally Came

The glimpses I gave online of my journey away from the evangelical theology of my youth were unsettling to a growing number of people in our church. Soon, a small group of people emerged who were deeply conservative and who held considerable political power in the church. This group, it seemed to me, spent hours every day watching my Facebook wall, ready to pounce if they didn't like something I posted.

Like the hovering seagulls we experience on the beach here in San Diego, relentless in their pursuit of abandoned sandwiches, Cheetos bags, and other unprotected food, these church members were waiting for me to let my guard down, to say or do something so egregious that they could oust me once and for all. Eventually, their gossip extended beyond their group as they brought their "concerns" to the attention of Pastor Jonathan, and on the evening of September 20, 2011, I left the mother lode of all sandwiches exposed on the beach blanket while I sauntered toward the shore. By the time I came back, the damage had been done and my fate had been sealed.

It was a Tuesday night, and I was home on the couch with my laptop open, scrolling through headlines on Yahoo[3] when one particular headline caught my eye. Don't Ask, Don't Tell had been repealed.

Waves of "this feels good . . . this feels right" coursed through me. I rejoiced that an established mechanism for discrimination, written into the laws of our country, had been rooted out. I clicked "Share Article," which opened

Facebook and offered me a chance to comment before I shared it.

Out came six words (yes, those six words): "I'm glad this day finally came."

I went to bed that night not thinking much about it. Not because I had any delusions that myriad others in my church community were also celebrating the repeal of DADT. But for me, at that time, the primary—if not sole—issue at stake with DADT was discrimination. I never considered the policy to be inherently connected to a person's belief about the rightness/wrongness of homosexuality. I remember assuming that there must be Christians out there who were against DADT purely on the basis of discrimination, even if they thought homosexuality was a sin.

Because in the Kingdom of God there is no place for discrimination, right?

Wrong.

As it turns out, for many evangelical Christians "no discrimination" doesn't apply to gay people. For reasons that go beyond the scope of this book, there is a unique brand of fear[4] in many Christians when it comes to homosexuality. Filled with outlandish negative stereotypes about the gay community, and asinine horror stories about the "gay agenda," many conservative Christians freak out when it comes to our LGBTQ siblings. And when I woke up the morning after DADT was repealed and checked my Facebook over a bowl of Frosted Mini-Wheats, I witnessed this freak-out firsthand.

"What's there to be glad about?"

"How can a Christian be pro-homosexuality?"

"Why is a pastor actively advancing the gay agenda?"

Anger and fear filled my news feed as people from my church reacted to my Facebook post from the previous night.

I didn't just wander to the edge of the ocean to dip my toes in. No, I spent hours in the waves while leaving a veritable feast uncovered on my blanket back on shore. By the time I returned, the gulls were stumbling away, unable to take flight because they'd gorged themselves so completely on the meal I recklessly left exposed.

Their watching and waiting had paid off.

Ugly Asterisks and a Situation

When I arrived at the church the next morning, Jonathan immediately called me to his office. He seemed weary for a Wednesday morning, and once he closed the door, I understood why.

His evening—and on into that morning—was a series of nonstop phone calls, text messages, and emails, all bemoaning my post. They demanded to know what was going to be done, some even suggesting that it was time to exercise the option to "terminate the young liberal." From the sound of it, the response from people on my Facebook page was but a fraction of the outcry launched toward Jonathan.

He cringed as he told me about the onslaught. Frustrated (at me? at the crowd? at the situation?), he asked me to remove the post. He hoped it would alleviate the tension and prevent more people from seeing it.

I ran it through my head: He wants me to remove a post that celebrates the end of discrimination against gay people from serving in the military?

It felt like an ugly asterisk on the whole "no discrimination in the Kingdom" thing.

When I got home, Kate and I talked ad nauseam about our growing sense of vexation with where we were at in life. The Naaman Effect no longer held any promise for peace. We had five years of roots planted in this community of fifteen hundred people, and yet those roots seemed a mile wide and an inch deep. It's obvious to me now, but I couldn't understand it then. Authenticity and vulnerability are the keys to connectivity. If you want to connect with others, truly connect, then you have to become known. You have to make yourself known. And Kate and I were investing so much energy in keeping ourselves hidden, not trusting people to know us. This, of course, would ensure that our efforts to connect with people would always hit a glass ceiling.

More than that, though, I had to face the reality that I was out of alignment. My internal convictions were expanding in directions that were not compatible with my environment, causing my external situation to deteriorate. The song of my soul was ready to experience some much-needed resolution, for it was long suspended in a perpetual dissonant chord, held together by nothing but the grace of God. It was evident that even when I wasn't intending to, my inner convictions were sneaking to the surface, daring to hope that they might be met with aligned external actions.

It was as though the past five years had been a slow inflation of a giant balloon. You know how the first 95 percent of a balloon blows up with no resistance, but the final 5 percent begs you to proceed with caution? And you sense you might have one small blow left before you stretch it beyond capacity. Sometimes I wonder if my subconscious, on that fateful Tuesday night, snuck its way to the surface and leaked out some of the air in my balloon labeled "internal convictions." As though it knew what my conscious self didn't: I was nearing the point of bursting. My out-of-alignment-ness had become too great for too long.

Those six words, "I'm glad this day finally came," closed the circle that opened back in March at Catalyst. In the same way that I stepped back from my sharpie confession, terrified but also wishing that someone would see what I wrote, perhaps my Facebook confession came from a similar place. My desire to be aligned finally became worth the risk of rejection.

That evening I received a phone call from Thomas, one of the elders. He told me that he had been away from his computer all day but that he had heard about the controversial post and wanted to hear my side. He also informed me that the chair of the elder board had called an emergency board meeting for Friday morning to "deal with the situation."

When you've moved from being a "pastor" to a "situation," rest assured it's not a good sign.

Coming Out of the Theological Closet

Was this how it would all end? I shuddered. After all these years of ministry, would they actually consider getting rid of me if they find out that I'm an affirming Christian? The thought seemed at once to be the most ridiculous and the most plausible scenario. As a friend of mine once said, the church can simultaneously be the safest and the most dangerous place.

Nowadays I don't think twice about declaring myself a straight ally of the LBGTQ community, but back then it was a terrifying prospect. I had no model to follow, community to lean on, or mentor to consult. And yet, amid the fog of uncertainty and fear, one truth kept easing back the clouds: it was time for me to come out of the theological closet.

I spent that Thursday afternoon pouring my heart and soul into a ten-page letter that explained my love for both the church and the elders on the board. It was a letter that mapped out my journey of rethinking our misuse of the Bible on homosexuality. I explained how I hadn't felt safe to share this with them sooner, but I hoped they could hear me now with open hearts and open minds. It was a letter that assured them of my commitment to not be divisive by teaching my opposing views at church or to try and persuade people toward my way of thinking.

Before I left for the day, I asked Jonathan and Sean (the other pastor on staff) if I could read them what I wrote. I wanted to practice coming out with the two guys I'd done ministry with for the past five years. It was nerve-racking; neither of them knew the full scope of my beliefs. And here

I was, stepping into a clear violation of "don't ask, don't tell." But my time for hiding was over. I wanted to tell, so badly, I wanted to tell. As much as I dreaded it, I dreaded the suffocating air of the theological closet more.

"Make yourselves comfortable, fellas, it's not a short letter," I joked, knowing that none of us was headed toward a state we'd call "comfort" any time soon.

The first few pages were read without incident, but I broke down when I got to the part where I implored them to keep in mind that I am a smart, well-read person, who studies Scripture with diligence. "I know it's something you appreciate about me," I said. I had to take a moment to breathe before I could move on. When I did, I pleaded with them to believe that I did not come to these conclusions lightly or quickly.

In the moment, I remember feeling confused that this part of the letter got me choked up: not the recounting of our years of ministry together, not the part where I told them how much I loved them and how much I loved my job and our church, but the part where I more or less said, "Fellas, I'm not dumb."

Looking back, I think I understand why my emotions spilled out in that moment. Even now, when people question my beliefs on this topic on social media, most assume I must be ignoring or disregarding the Bible in order to arrive at the conclusions I do. Or that I've checked my brains in an effort to be more loving and tolerant. Or that I've given in to the pressures of the world, succumbing to the culture around me. Or that I am trying to justify the actions of a close friend or family member.

But here is the thing: when I went through the process of studying the Clobber Passages I wasn't trying to justify the life of a family member or friend. I wasn't, as is often assumed, trying to make sense of someone I knew who was gay and Christian. At that time, I barely even knew any gay people. And I certainly didn't have any gay friends or know anyone who was gay and Christian. I wasn't bending my views to give in to the pressures of the world or taking the supposed "easy" way out. Heck, the easy way would have been to ignore what I was learning, ignore the convictions stirring within me, ignore the work of the Spirit in my life, and stick with the status quo. Most important, I was not disregarding the Bible. If anything, I was paying *more* attention. I saw the Clobber Passages with fresh eyes, and I discovered how the church had been misusing certain portions of the Bible.

I think the tears came at that part in the letter because I was desperate for my two friends to see me.

To see me as someone who cared enough about this to take it seriously.

To see me as someone who was following Christ as best as I knew how, even if it meant going to unpopular places.

To see me as someone who was sincere in my efforts to align my head with my heart.

I can only imagine how it must feel for an LGBTQ person to come out of the actual closet: Desperate to be seen. To be heard. To be trusted. To be accepted. To be loved.

Sensing Jonathan and Sean's anxiety as I was nearing the end, I turned the final page, read the last paragraph, and slowly set the letter down with trembling hands. My insides were churning, but I had done it. I had spoken aloud my words of affirmation for the LGBTQ community. The closet doors had been rent aside, and I was standing outside them—barely standing perhaps, but standing nonetheless. As anxious as I was about what would happen next, there was also a massive part of me that sighed in relief. It would seem that once again I was "glad this day had finally come."

With trepidation I lifted my eyes to see their reaction. I had a hunch this would be no surprise to Sean. He and I had talked before, about other ideas and theological issues, to the point where I'm sure he could have guessed what I believed. But Jonathan? How would he respond?

His eyes seemed unable to look up and meet my own as he placed the letter on the coffee table. With defeat in his voice he said, "If you read this tomorrow, this will be a resignation letter."

It wasn't a threat. It wasn't said with malice or disgust. It was just matter of fact. He knew, as did I, that the contents of this letter, revealing myself as a welcoming and affirming ally for the LGBTQ community, would place me too far outside the camp of our church's brand of Christianity.

He then went on to share his own thoughts on homosexuality. The intensity of his convictions surprised me. I assumed we disagreed, but even I wasn't prepared for just how much. Finally, he looked at me. Or, more accurately, he looked *through* me, as though I had become unfamiliar to him—a stranger he no longer knew. I so desperately wanted to shake him and say, "It's still me! I'm here! Don't be afraid!"

That was the first time regret showed up. If that's what it looked like to make yourself known, that the people you love no longer recognize you, then I wasn't sure I wanted in. Somehow my efforts to finally be seen had left me feeling invisible.

Unity, Liberty, and Charity

Exhausted, the three of us bid one another adieu. I left heartbroken and dismayed that my friends didn't have my back. I realized they disagreed with me, and I had no desire or delusion that I could convince them otherwise. But deep inside I had hoped that I might witness the elusive concept often preached from the pulpit but rarely lived out. I'm referring to that quote, often misattributed to Saint Augustine, "In the essentials, unity; in the nonessentials, liberty; in all things, charity."[5]

It seemed absurd to me, when considering historical reference points such as the ancient creeds or the work of early church fathers and mothers, to think of sexuality as an "essential doctrine of the faith." And yet, for the current age of the church, it has become a litmus test, defining whether you are in or out of most Christian circles. Perhaps I was naive, but I hoped that we could find a way to transcend such binary options. I dared imagine that the church leadership would extend liberty to me as I held an opinion foreign to theirs and that together we could practice charity in our continued efforts to love God, grow together, and serve the world.

But as I lay down to sleep that night—or, rather, lay idly in bed . . . I don't recall much sleeping—I felt in my gut that neither liberty nor charity would be mine the next morning.

They wanted only unity—nay, uniformity—and this time I had gone too far.

CHAPTER 4

→

REFRAMING THE STORY OF SODOM

Genesis 19

I was simultaneously mesmerized and terrified when I first saw *Jurassic Park*. I was eleven years old when it came out in 1993, but as much as I loved it, I haven't watched it since . . . until the other night.

Over the past twenty-plus years, I haven't thought about *Jurassic Park* all that often, but when I did, I remembered only three things about the movie: The scene with ripples in the glass of water when the T-Rex shows up; the idea that DNA could be extracted from a sap-trapped mosquito (convincing myself and countless other children that the story was plausible); and the scene where velociraptors jump on kitchen counters to hunt people. Sure, I could tell you that, generally speaking, the movie was about a theme park full of dinosaurs that escaped their pens and wreaked havoc, but when I rewatched the movie as a thirty-three-year old, I realized how many plot points and characters I had missed or forgotten about: Investors wanted to back out of the park? One of the employees tried to smuggle out dino DNA? Samuel L. Jackson was in this movie?

Do you know what I'm talking about? Have you ever experienced that with a movie or a book you haven't read in years? You might remember the overall concept of the story, but you are shocked at how many details you forgot or missed?

This was my experience when I began my research into the Clobber Passages and chose Genesis 19 as my starting point. The story of the destruction of Sodom and Gomorrah, like *Jurassic Park*, was a story that, in terms of the big picture, I could decently recite. Two cities, back in the days of Abraham, were so wicked that God destroyed them with fireballs from heaven. Oh, and something about Lot's wife turning into a salt statue. But when I sat down to study it for the first time in years, I couldn't believe what I was reading.

I wonder how many other well-intentioned Christians haven't looked at Genesis 19 in a while, leaving them with nothing more than a vague sense of, "That's the story about God destroying cities because of homosexuality, right?"

Wrong.

It's time to revisit this ancient story, a story that, unfortunately, has been misused as a warning against the depravity of homosexuality, patterned with divine retribution if humanity ignores said warning.

Did Fire Really Rain Down?

A full treatment of the destruction of Sodom and Gomorrah is beyond the scope of this book. My hope, instead, is to evaluate whether or not Genesis 19 can offer any reasonable evidence that the Bible condemns gay people or prohibits people of the same sex from enjoying a loving, committed, and consensual relationship. But there are some important considerations before jumping in.

For instance, the way you approach stories in the Old Testament will influence how you read, interpret, and apply Genesis 19. Do you begin with the assumption that Genesis is a literal, fly-on-the-wall account of ancient people and stories? Do you see the stories in Genesis as myth, historical, or some combination of both? Do you read stories from the first portion of Genesis (chapters 1–12), such as the garden of Eden, tower of Babel, and the flood, differently than the rest of Genesis (13–50), from Abraham onward? Those sorts of questions are more than can be covered in this chapter. As for me, I don't believe that Genesis was written with the goal of keeping a literal word-for-word account of the history of Israel. I do not read dialogue and expect it to be precisely what was said five thousand years ago. I do not read descriptions of events and think, "If we had a dash cam attached to a donkey, then that is exactly how it would have played out." That is an anachronistic approach for how the ancient world thought about, and went about, recording the memories and stories of previous generations.

So one of the main questions I ask when it comes to a story like the destruction of Sodom and Gomorrah is not, "How did that event literally take place?" but "Why was that story told and retold over campfires from generation to generation for hundreds of years until it was finally written down and preserved?"

When it comes to the Sodom and Gomorrah story as it is told in Genesis 18:16–19:29, I ask questions such as: "What does this story have to say to or about people who are not straight?" "What does it have to offer same-sex couples who are looking for divine wisdom or blessing regarding the sanctity of their relationship?" And so on.

As with my rediscovery of *Jurassic Park*, you may be surprised at what's in store.

And now, a story . . .

Stories and Virtues in the Ancient World

Two foreigners arrive late one night to a town whose reputation for wickedness is well-known. The foreigners receive shelter and provisions at one home in particular, highlighting the stark contrast between the host and the rest of the wicked town. The two foreigners reveal to their hospitable hosts that they have come that night on a divine mission to destroy the town. However, due to the generous hospitality shown them, the two foreigners want to save their hosts and urge them to leave town immediately, not looking back as they go. When the escaping family crosses the borders of town, they glance behind them and witness the utter destruction of the entire city and all the wicked occupants therein.

Recognize that story?

Though it sounds like the story of Sodom and Gomorrah in Genesis 19, it is actually the story of Baucis and Philemon as told by the Roman poet, Ovid, in his masterpiece, *Metamorphoses*. The two foreigners were Zeus and Hermes, who disguised themselves as ordinary peasants and were rejected by the wicked people in the town but received by Baucis and Philemon. These two hosts were the embodiment of the pious posture of hospitality, one of the ancient world's most cherished virtues. The Greeks even had a term for this, *xenia*, which meant "guest-friendship." It shows up as a central theme in many ancient stories. (The opposite of friendship to guests, fear of guests, would hence be *xenophobia*.) The notion of opening your home and sharing your resources for the betterment of a traveler, stranger, or foreigner, was imperative. Failing to do so was tragic and shameful. Stories and traditions—like Baucis and Philemon, and like Sodom and Gomorrah—were passed on as a way to convey the severe consequences of inhospitality. You never know if the person you reject just might be a god in human form. Or, as the author of Hebrews would come to say it, "Do not neglect to show hospitality to strangers, for thereby some have entertained angels unawares" (Heb. 13:2 ESV).

What does all this tell me about the story in Genesis 19? It makes me feel that whether or not the events in Genesis 19 literally happened may not matter when it comes to understanding why the story was preserved in Israel's history. It is but one of multiple ancient accounts just like it; and the purpose of all of them is to highlight the importance of hospitality. So we should not be surprised if the story of the destruction of Sodom and Gomorrah holds similar details and themes.

Contrasting Postures

Let's begin in Genesis 18, which parallels—and sets the stage for—the opening of Genesis 19. Abraham is sitting at the entrance of his tent when he looks up and sees three men, whom the storyteller says are the Lord and the two messengers who would eventually wander down to Sodom and Gomorrah. Upon seeing them, Abraham greets them, bows before them, and invites them to his place for food, drink, and relaxation. This is quintessential hospitality: greeting, welcoming, and hosting with food and shelter.

The storyteller then recounts a fascinating conversation between Abraham and God where God debates whether or not to tell Abraham of the plan to destroy Sodom and Gomorrah. God decides to rope Abraham in and then makes a striking contrast between God's plans for the tribes of Abraham's descendants versus the tribes of those who live in Sodom and Gomorrah. Israel will become a moral and just nation, a blessing to all other nations. In Sodom and Gomorrah, on the other hand, "The cries of injustice . . . are countless, and their sin is very serious!" (Gen. 18:20). Right away, the storyteller wants us to know that whatever is going on in Sodom and Gomorrah is so corrupt, so horrendous, so *not* moral and just, that it gets the attention of the God-who-hears-the-cries-of-the-oppressed. Future generations are meant to be reminded of these contrasting postures. Israel is called to become a great nation, moral and upright, so that they can bless others. Directly opposite are the unjust and wicked ways of other peoples, aka Sodom and Gomorrah. This theme will come up again when we discuss the Clobber Passages in Leviticus.

With the contrast established, the storyteller then tells of an extraordinary back and forth between Abraham and God, as Abraham pleads with God to spare the cities. He actually pushes back against God, as if to suggest that he is more compassionate than the Divine. With brazen negotiating tactics, Abraham convinces God to let the wicked cities live if but ten innocent people can be found. Apparently, they could not.

The storyteller wants us to understand that the situation in Sodom and Gomorrah has gotten so bad that God feels intervention is the only option (echoing the flood story from Genesis 6). We are also meant to see a clear juxtaposition between people who follow God and people who don't. Abraham demonstrates both hospitality and compassion, as he welcomes the Lord to his tent and then bargains for the safety of his nephew's adopted hometown. This posture, modeled by Abraham for the sake of future generations, stands in stark contrast to what we are about to witness from the depraved pagans of Sodom and Gomorrah.

Destruction of Sodom and Gomorrah

Chapter 19 opens much the same way as chapter 18. The two messengers (or angels) arrive in Sodom at night and are greeted by Lot, who sits at the gates of the city.

> The two messengers entered Sodom in the evening. Lot, who was sitting at the gate of Sodom, saw them, got up to greet them, and bowed low. He said, "Come to your servant's house, spend the night, and

wash your feet. Then you can get up early and go on your way."

But they said, "No, we will spend the night in the town square." He pleaded earnestly with them, so they went with him and entered his house. He made a big meal for them, even baking unleavened bread, and they ate." (Gen. 19:1–3)

According to the timeline in Genesis, Lot has probably been in Sodom for about twenty years at this point, and it is not a large city. Archaeologists have dug up several sites suggesting that Sodom and Gomorrah were cities of around one thousand people each. So we can assume that Lot is well informed regarding his hometown. He knows the people, the culture, and the essential happenings of Sodom. Therefore, when the storyteller places Lot at the gate when the messengers arrive (likely meaning he is on gatekeeper duty that night), we should not be surprised by Lot "pleading earnestly" that the visitors stay with him. Why? Well, this certainly isn't the first time outsiders showed up late and sought shelter at Sodom, only to be met by people so wicked that God thinks it best to eradicate them altogether.

Just like Abraham, Lot's posture to the messengers is to greet them, bow before them, and immediately offer them food and shelter. The messengers accept Lot's offer of hospitality, which includes a warm place to spend the night and a large meal to fill their bellies. But just before turndown service, the conflict emerges.

Before they went to bed, the men of the city of Sodom — everyone from the youngest to the oldest — surrounded the house and called to Lot, "Where are the men who arrived tonight?" (Gen. 19:4–5a)

Lot's attempt to save these visitors from the men of the city doesn't work. Word has gotten out that two strangers have shown up, late at night, and Lot—the resident immigrant, the outsider of the group—has swept them away to his own house.

Do you notice how the storyteller points out that every man in the city shows up at Lot's house? Several times, in fact, this detail is highlighted. This should rule out, right off the bat, any interpretation that this story is about homosexual orientation or same-sex attraction. It simply cannot be the case that every man in Sodom, from the youngest to the oldest, was gay. Common sense (and statistics) tell us this. So if this is not a hoard of gay men overcome with desire to have sex with two out-of-towners, then who were they? Let's keep going with the story, and see what the storyteller wants us to know about them.

> "Bring them out to us so that we may have sex with them."
>
> Lot went out toward the entrance, closed the door behind him, and said, "My brothers, don't do such an evil thing." (Gen. 19:5b–7)

The mob of men, young and old, pound on Lot's door and demand that he give up the two men inside because they want to have sex with them. This translation is overly gracious, implying a desire to do something "with" the men. But make no mistake about it, consent or mutuality is not on the mob's mind. They want to do something *to* the men. To put it bluntly, they intend to gang rape the visitors. This was, in the ancient world, how you showed your dominance over and against the outsider and the enemy.[1] It was not about homoerotic desire; it was about dishonoring the other and stripping them of their masculinity, and thereby their humanity. So just as the detail in the story about all the men surrounding Lot's house tells us this story can't be about judgment against homosexuality as an orientation or same-sex attraction, the point about the mob's plans to gang rape, humiliate, and subject the visitors to such displays of dominance also tells us that this can't be a story about same-sex love or a relationship between two people of the same sex. To ask Genesis 19 to weigh in on the questions of a biblical posture toward same-sex attraction or the sinfulness of a loving, committed same-sex relationship, is to ask questions it simply does not (and cannot) answer.

Lot, panicking that his fears are coming to fruition and desperate to protect his guests and uphold the sanctity of hospitality, then says this,

> "I've got two daughters who are virgins. Let me bring them out to you, and you may do to them whatever you wish. But don't do anything to these men because they are now under the protection of my roof." (Gen. 19:8)

I don't think the point in this part of the story, where Lot shamefully offers up his two virgin daughters for the pleasure of the mob, is intended for us to think, "Oh, I guess they really didn't care about women back then." Even though that is true (in that patriarchal world women were seen as property), this detail of the story is meant to illustrate the extreme measures to which Lot is willing to go to succeed in his efforts at hospitality. This is not a statement against the value of a woman, but a statement for the value of hospitality. It is supposed to shock us. We should be bothered by such a heinous idea. But we are then supposed to carry it out to its logical conclusion by considering *how much more* hospitality is to be connected to pious and upright living.

Plus—if you're keeping score on details that point to this not being a story about homosexuality—it's fair to assume that, if all these men are gay (anachronistically speaking, of course), Lot will not bother offering two women to them as a consolation. But he does, and, of course, they are not interested. Their presence at Lot's house that evening is not about sexual desire. They are not looking to have a good time with the two men from out of town; so they are not interested in Lot's daughters either. They have surrounded Lot's house, demanding to have sex with the two messengers, for the sake of control and power. But most of all, they are there so that the storyteller can show what the opposite of hospitality looks like. Abraham and Lot? They understand how to be people of kindness, compassion, and hospitality. Sodom and Gomorrah? They are notoriously wicked people who care nothing for the merits of the ancient practice of hospitality.

> They said, "Get out of the way!" And they continued, "Does this immigrant want to judge us? Now we will hurt you more than we will hurt them." They pushed Lot back and came close to breaking down the door. The men inside reached out and pulled Lot back into the house with them and slammed the door. Then the messengers blinded the men near the entrance of the house, from the youngest to the oldest, so that they groped around trying to find the entrance.
> The men said to Lot, "Who's still with you here? Take away from this place your sons-in-law, your sons, your daughters, and everyone else you have in the city because we are about to destroy this place. The LORD has found the cries of injustice so serious that the LORD sent us to destroy it." (Gen. 19:9–13)

The mob is relentless in their pursuit, now threatening to exact violence on Lot, who is also an outsider. This further shows Sodom's contempt for those unlike themselves. The story ends with the messengers warning Lot—just as Zeus and Hermes did for Baucis and Philemon—to take his family and leave town immediately because they are about to destroy the city. Lot tries to convince his sons-in-law to flee, but they think he is joking. So Lot, his wife, and his two daughters are the sole survivors after the Lord "rained down burning asphalt from the skies"

(v. 24), leveling for all time the wicked cities of Sodom and Gomorrah.[2]

The Testimony of the Rest of Scripture

Now to return to the two questions I asked at the beginning of this chapter. First, why might it be that this was one of the few stories retold generation after generation and preserved in Scripture? Second, what does it have to say about homosexuality? Both questions can be answered with a high degree of certainty.

If Genesis 19 was Scripture's only mention of Sodom and Gomorrah, it could perhaps be reasonable to believe that one of the sins (perhaps even *the* sin) of the decimated cities was related to sexual immorality (if, of course, we ignore the observations about how gang rape is about power and not sexual desire). However, both the Old Testament and New Testament weigh in on the sin of Sodom, giving us all the insight we might need as to why that story was preserved and what it meant. We don't have to work too hard to interpret the story of the destruction of Sodom and Gomorrah, because prophets like Isaiah, Ezekiel, Jeremiah, and then Jesus himself, all do it for us.

In the days of Isaiah, the people of God had desperately lost their way. According to Isaiah, Israel's worship had become meaningless. This caused them to neglect doing good, such as seeking justice, defending the oppressed, and tending to orphans and widows. This prompted Isaiah to warn his people, "If the LORD of heavenly forces had not spared a few of us, / we would be like Sodom" (Isa. 1:9), and bluntly calling Israel's leaders, "leaders of Sodom" (v. 10).

Jeremiah lamented about the prophets in his day, specifically calling out their adulterous ways and their incessant lying about visions and dreams. Worst of all, they neglected the most important job of a prophet: calling people to repentance. Like Isaiah before him, Jeremiah compared his people to Sodom and Gomorrah, "In the prophets of Jerusalem / I saw something horrible: / . . . . / In my eyes, they are no better than Sodom; / its people are like Gomorrah" (Jer. 23:14).

Ezekiel gives us the clearest window into how the memory of Sodom and Gomorrah played itself out in Jewish consciousness. Once again, the two ancient cities are used as a measuring stick to describe how bad life had gotten with the Israelite people. According to Ezekiel, Jerusalem had become, in the eyes of God, even more detestable and depraved than that old ash heap known as Sodom. "'Now this was the sin of your sister Sodom: She and her daughters were arrogant, overfed and unconcerned; they did not help the poor and needy. They were haughty and did detestable things before me. Therefore I did away with them as you have seen'" (Ezek. 16:49–50 NIV). As far as Ezekiel saw it, it was not sexual immorality (let alone homosexuality or same-sex sex acts) that brought down the fire from heaven.

According to the prophets, then, when the Hebrew people thought of Sodom and Gomorrah, they did not think of them in terms of cities that were wicked as a result of men wanting to have sex with other men. No, the sins of Sodom were based on the fact that they had plenty of resources but did not open themselves up to those who were in need. In short, they were notoriously inhospitable.

Finally, Jesus himself stood in the Jewish tradition of seeing Sodom and Gomorrah as historical examples of the wickedness of rejecting the outsider. When he sent out his twelve disciples to go from town to town proclaiming the arrival of the Kingdom of God, he said, "If anyone refuses to welcome you or listen to your words, shake the dust off your feet as you leave that house or city. I assure you that it will be more bearable for the land of Sodom and Gomorrah on Judgment Day than it will be for that city" (Matt. 10:14–15).

I realize it may feel like a stretch to our Western-modern minds to think of inhospitality in this way: a sin so egregious that people would believe God destroyed entire cities over it; so heinous that it is on par with activities like lying, adultery, and idolatry. But we must do our best to listen to ancient stories (both in the Bible and outside it) that insist that hospitality, or "guest-friendship," was held in such regard. If someone told a tale of morality to illustrate what inhospitality looks like, you would expect the story to sound like Genesis 19, or like Baucis and Philemon. In other words, while we might read Genesis 19 and get stuck on the idea of men wanting to have sex with other men—and therefore think it's a story about sex—for the ancient consciousness, this would have been the most logical way to illustrate how inhospitable the people of Sodom and Gomorrah were.

In the end, when read with fresh eyes, noticing all the little details as well as paying attention to the larger themes the storyteller is utilizing, this story can be UnClobbered with relative ease. This is not a story about gay men, especially since the concept of "sexual orientation" would have been completely foreign back then. But more than that, it's not a story about men who are sexually attracted to other men. The passion of the mob banging down Lot's door was motivated by a desire to exercise control over the two men, not because they wanted to enjoy same-sex sex acts with them, or develop a relationship with them. We have to be able to see that plot point for what it is, and then move past it to understand the story as a whole.

Ancient Israel was uniquely called by God to be a reflection of the Lord back into the world. God was going to bless them so that they could be a blessing to others. They were to operate categorically different from the nations around them, including (but not limited to) how they opened themselves up to the stranger, the alien, the foreigner, and the immigrant. They were to be a people who embodied hospitality, sought justice for the oppressed, cared for the outcast, and used their abundance to provide for others.

The destruction of Sodom and Gomorrah functioned in the life of Israel as a story to remind them of the dangers of forgetting their calling. Abraham and Lot were held up, exemplars of hospitality, in stark contrast to the debased power mongers of Sodom and Gomorrah who viewed outsiders as objects to control and exploit.

Although, historically, Genesis 19 has been on the list of Clobber Passages, it appears that trend is changing. I have noticed a shift in how non-affirming Christians handle this story. While they still maintain that the other Clobber Passages articulate a biblical position against same-sex relationships, they acknowledge that Genesis 19 is unhelpful to that end.[3] Someone would have to ignore all other ancient stories and references to hospitality that mirror Genesis 19, and they would have to reject the interpretive words of Isaiah, Jeremiah, Ezekiel, and Jesus, in order to maintain a position that insists Sodom and Gomorrah has anything to do with homosexuality.

Instead, what if we learned from our misuse of this Clobber Passage and instead took to heart the real message of the story of Sodom and Gomorrah? Historically this passage has been seen as evidence for a God who opposes homosexuality so ardently that God would destroy entire cities as a result. It has been a story used to separate the LGBTQ community from the rest of the flock, to keep them as outsiders. And yet, when understood properly, the entire point of Genesis 19 is that the people of God are called to be people who receive the outcast and the outsiders, not create them.

What if this story became a rallying point for calling the church back to the importance of hospitality? Of greeting people who are outside, embracing them, and leading them inside for nourishment and rest?

That's a pretty powerful place to start when it comes to homosexuality and the Bible.

CHAPTER 5

→

UNFIT TO BE A PASTOR

Waiting Rooms

Our minivan idled through the church parking lot, quieter than usual since we left the boys at home. Normally on Fridays the lot would be vacant, but that morning it held half a dozen cars, property of the arrived-and-waiting elder board. The emergency meeting, assembled to deal with me and my situation, was minutes away from commencing. Even as the curb kissed our front tires, announcing our arrival, I hesitated to kill the engine—in part because I wanted to let the song on the radio finish, but I think I was also delaying the inevitable.

As I sat in the driver's seat, taking in the lyrics, I noticed they had a calming effect, like when a roller coaster ends and you begin to breathe again as your heart rate normalizes. Leeland Mooring, the front man for *Leeland*, was singing about the love of God, and how he was afraid that he wouldn't know how to receive it. Instead, he just falls down in awe and wonder.

Me? I was afraid too. But it wasn't the fear Leeland sang of—the fear of feeling small and inadequate in the face of such heavy and beautiful grace. No, my fear was that the ensuing meeting would be heartbreakingly absent of such love and grace.

I let Leeland finish, inhaled slowly, locked eyes with Kate, and reached for the door handle.

Do you remember going to the doctor when you were young? For me, and many others in my generation, the intimidating waiting room was made a little less scary by the stacks of *Highlights* magazines, tinted yellow from being piled on the coffee table under the sun. Nothing distracted me from my anxiety about seeing Dr. Conklin more effectively than searching for hidden objects, admiring the artwork of seven-year-olds around the country, and practicing my sleuthing skills by discovering the slight differences between two nearly identical photos.

But this wasn't Dr. Conklin's office, and there were no *Highlights* magazines.

So what do you do while you're waiting to be summoned for a meeting you know will forever shape the course of your vocational—and for me, personal—life?

You play ping pong, of course.

The Final Moments

When Kate and I were told that the elders were not ready for me, we meandered toward the youth building and hung out with Sean, attempting to pretend it was just another day. This was almost achievable around Sean. Even though he and I could not have been more different, we nonetheless had a bond that transcended trivialities such as theological agreement or political sameness. And though he wasn't on the board (so he wouldn't be in the meeting), he made sure to come to church early that morning just to be present with Kate and me.

He and I scooped up a couple of paddles and rummaged to find a ball. While we mindlessly rallied on the beaten-down table in the high-school room, Kate sat on one of those classic we-don't-want-this-anymore-so-let's-give-it-to-the-youth-group couches. Her face was steely, holding the courage that I was lacking, as though she knew that no matter what was about to happen it would not change who she was or who we were. I tried to draw from her silent strength as I spun backhands across the table, but I couldn't stop thinking about how I might go to bed that night a radically different person than when I had woken up. The heaviness was starting to sink in.

Looking back now, I can see how I had unintentionally allowed my identity to be shaped during my seven years in full-time ministry. The only me that I knew was "pastor." And yet, what if my position on homosexuality would deem me unfit to be one any longer? Who would I be if I weren't a pastor?

Smash. A winning forehand down the sideline should have made me smile. It always makes me smile. It's my favorite move. But no smiles came to me that day.

I heard footsteps outside. Daylight painted the floor as someone pulled the metal double doors back and entered the room just as Sean was retrieving the ball I smashed. The paddle in my shaking hands and the table top collided as I set it down, more violently than I intended. I watched Jonathan enter the room and searched his eyes for some indication of what might be coming.

"Hey Colby, they are ready for you," he said in hushed tones. He didn't look optimistic, and I couldn't help but notice his use of the third person, as though to put distance between himself and the rest of the elders.

I wrapped my arms around Kate, not wanting to let go, and was conscious of how the bump in her stomach added itself to our embrace. Seven months pregnant with our fourth son, Kate's belly struck me with another tangible reminder of what was at stake.

Arizona was the sure thing. It offered a paycheck. It had a house that we built and raised three sons in, with a doctor we trusted to deliver baby number four. Though it had only been five years, for us, it was the longest we'd lived together anywhere. Arizona was our life.

That future was available to me, and I knew it. As I released Kate, I considered how I could walk in there, as Sean had brainstormed the day before, and talk my way out of this. My "coming out of the theological closet" letter could stay in my backpack, unread. I could receive their criticism of my Facebook etiquette and apologize. I could respond to their questions about my theology with answers nebulous enough to maintain employment. I knew that I could secure the security, if I truly wanted to.

But as we looked each other in the eye, my hand grazing her belly, the vision of a future where I continued to not be known, to not be integrated, faded like the house on shifting sand that it was. That was not the way forward, and I knew it. Security isn't the goal. It *can't* be the goal. It likes to persuade us that it is, but it's a lie. The goals are integrity, wholeness, and alignment, and I was so close. My internal convictions could see the faint light of external reality. I thought, maybe this is what Jesus meant by, "Those who lose their lives . . . shall find them" (see Luke 9:24).

So I picked up my bag, stuffed with eight copies of my ten-page letter, and followed Jonathan out the door. As we walked through the courtyard toward the church offices, he filled the silence between us.

"I never wanted this to happen . . . I never dreamed this would happen. . . ."

The sun shines every day in Arizona, and that morning was no exception. Ten o'clock in the morning and it was already 92 degrees out. The temperature would soon reach 108. It was a short walk across the courtyard, but I was already sweating. I'm sure my nerves exacerbated the assault of the desert air.

It was sad walking into that meeting behind Jonathan, because I got the sense that once we got in there, Jonathan would not be behind me. Most of my life I have been starved for the voice of affirmation and love that many people say comes only from a father. For the five years we'd worked together, Jonathan filled that void more than I could have asked for.

"Yeah," I mumbled, "same here."

No Going Back

Frank was in his early fifties, stood just north of five feet tall, shaved his head bald, wore a white goatee and wire-rimmed glasses, and was always smiling. He was a pharmaceutical salesman, giving him years of experience in being charming and persuasive. Before he was elected as chair of the elder board, Frank was a close friend. It was Frank who showed up the day our moving van rolled in to Arizona and helped us unload it in the 117-degree weather and then came back several hours later with three dozen hangers and extra speaker wire for my surround sound. It was Frank who volunteered countless hours to serve behind the scenes in the worship ministry and then took months of guitar lessons to fill a gap in our worship band. It was Frank who traveled to Liberia, Africa, with me to play concerts at outreach events in cities and villages across the war-torn country.

But when he acquired the title of "chair," I felt a shift. We all noticed it. Not everyone was as concerned about it as I was, probably because no one was hiding as many liberal skeletons as I was. Frank was a hardcore conservative who, I think, believed it was his calling to keep the church from falling down the rabbit hole of the social gospel,[1] a path that (in his mind) led to anti-Christian theology. Now granted, he never lost his warm heart and kind smile, but over the course of the last year, he had seemed less and less interested in serving the body or loving his neighbor, and more interested in preserving "truth" and rooting out what he considered to be bad doctrine.

And now here we were. Frank had been part of the "concerned" group I mentioned earlier, and now he was leading the charge to get rid of me. I wondered what happened to my old friend.

"Colby," his naturally raspy voice began, "we want to hear your position on homosexuality as a sin, and whether or not you believe that homosexual marriage is something that should be considered normal or acceptable?"

No sooner had I sat in the lone vacant chair, completing the circle of eight men crammed into Jonathan's office, than the inquisition began. And those were the first words spoken. Not, "Hi Colby," or "Thanks for coming in today," or "How about that Cardinals game yesterday, huh?" There would be no small talk. No breaking of the ice or easing in.

I took in the question and surveyed the room. I noticed the large wooden giraffe in the corner of Jonathan's office, the one he brought back from one of his trips to Africa. He grew up in Africa, and most of his family still lived there. Every year, Jonathan would lead mission trips back to his home country, putting shoes on bare African feet, leading free medical clinics, and helping women to find respect and equality. As I stared at the hand-carved animal, she reminded me why I loved this place. For all its flaws, our church had so many incredible Kingdom-fulfilling attributes about it.

Then I looked at the men in the room. Half of them were staring at me, the other half down at the floor. Were they ashamed to be here? Embarrassed to look me in the eye, because somewhere deep inside they knew there was something wrong about this whole ordeal?

"Can I ask you why that question is so important?" I Socratically replied. But I wasn't just being cute; I was interested in the reasoning behind their deep angst about the possibility that I might not see homosexuality as they did. What was at stake for these men? Were the rumors true, that some of the largest givers might leave the church if it employed an open and affirming pastor? Were there other staff members who might resign because they couldn't work with me? Did the elders see homosexuality as a genuine threat to the purity of the gospel?

What was it? Why this emergency meeting? Why this panic?

Frank responded, "Because we live in an environment where conservative Christians feel assaulted. Society and our government are forcing things down our throats. So I think we need to know where our leaders stand on this issue."

His answer sounded ridiculous to me, but the reality is that he's not alone. There are many Christians for whom this is important because they have bought into a narrative of fear: fear that there is a war against Christians; and homosexuality is the weapon du jour.

Before I answered, I looked from elder to elder, one at a time, and asked if they agreed with Frank.

"Is it that important to you that I share my theology on homosexuality; when our church doesn't have a position on it, and we've never asked past or potential employees about it?"

Each one said yes.

Then Frank added, "I think it's extremely clear what the Scriptures say. You cannot stand on a platform of the church and espouse redemption, or partnering with God to bring the Kingdom on earth as it is in heaven, and at the same time say that homosexuality—as corrupt as it is— should be accepted as normal behavior. For a majority of Christians, this issue is that important."

His words hung in the air, like the unexpected ember that floats up from a campfire, demanding attention as it swirls in front of you. Jonathan attempted to shift the energy of the room away from hostility and said in his soft-est voice, "Colby, I think maybe you could help by shar-ing your heart behind your post from Tuesday. And then, maybe the most clarifying thing would be to answer for us, *is homosexuality a sin?*"

All the heads of the elders pivoted toward me, perhaps hoping that I would help make this meeting swift and their decision easy. My five years of doing ministry with these men and their families, though, felt too significant to me. I felt as though it required that I at least do my part to elevate the conversation. If these were our final moments together, I wanted to ensure that nothing was left unsaid. And dumbing it down to an answer to one question—about the "sinfulness of homosexuality"—felt like crude neglect of community and relationship, not to mention a betrayal of the totality of my convictions.

When I was younger, I used to love diving from the tall-est diving board at our local pool. Mastering the technique on the smaller diving board came easily, but mustering the courage to attempt such a feat from three times the height was another story. To get it right, every part of the process had to synch up: the acceleration of the approach, initiat-ing the jump from the correct location so that you catch the end of the board and maximize the spring, timing the grad-ual forward turn of your body—too slow and you belly flop, too fast and you land on your back, both of which are no fun from ten feet up. But the key is committing . . . all the way. Once you take that first step toward the end of the board, you have to execute. Any attempt to bail, at any stage in the process, guarantees that the entire pool hears your failure—the sound of smacking flesh reverberating off the concrete walls.

The boys were at home. The van was parked. Kate was waiting outside. Ping pong had been played. And there I sat with my letter in hand.

There was no going back.

The Letter

I passed around my ten-page letter and asked the men to indulge me while I read it, requesting they resist the urge to jump ahead to the end. I didn't want them to find just one sentence that satiated their desire to know my theology. It was important to me that they heard my heart in all of this and listened as I walked them through my process of becoming an affirming Christian.

I swallowed before I started reading, unsure if I'd do so again until after the last page.

The letter began with gratitude for my years on staff, amazed that they entrusted an entire Worship and Arts Ministry to a twenty-four-year-old kid from Oregon. Then I apologized for stirring up controversy on Facebook, and for how it disrupted their week. I was honest about feeling targeted by a small-but-vocal group in the church. Then I said how it hurt to realize that my years of ministry there didn't seem to matter if what people suspected was true — that I was okay with gay people.

Two pages then spoke directly to each board member. I told each elder what I loved and admired about them. I recounted stories of shared ministry. And I described how they had each made a lasting impact in my life.

Then, after the appeal to our histories had been made, I said the following:

Do you believe that I have been sincere, true and faithful? Do you believe that my heart and love for Jesus is authentic? I ask you these things because I feel it important to keep in mind who I am as a person and who I have been as a pastor here. Because that has been the real me. And it's also important to me that you hear how someone like that, someone like me, can at the same time hold beliefs that are outside the confines of Western conservative evangelical Christianity.

Without looking up, and only halfway through my letter, my heart was growing heavy. It wasn't nerves I felt, like I assumed I would. It was despair. The energy in the room, with each page turn, created a strange barrier between me and the elders. I could tell they weren't buying what I was selling. Which I guess was part of the problem—I wasn't selling anything. I wasn't trying to convince them of my views or convict them of theirs.

Next, I talked about my thinking behind the events from Tuesday night. I explained how, for me, DADT was an issue of discrimination, independent of my personal feelings about sexuality. I tried to show how it wasn't unreasonable for me to think that other Christians—maybe even some in our own church—were also celebrating the repeal. "It's possible," I said, "to think that homosexuality is sin but also believe that discrimination against the gay community and treating our LGBTQ brothers, sisters, and siblings like second-class citizens is not okay. I know this, because that was me for a number of years."

Finally, I used the last few pages to share how I'd come to believe that we have misused the Bible on homosexuality. I talked about the theological journey I had been on, following the Spirit as best as I knew how. Then I gave a few thoughts about how I approach the Clobber Passages, all while repeatedly assuring them that my goal was not to argue or try and convince them or anyone else in the church of my views. I wrapped it all up with these words:

> So after nine pages of me pouring out my heart I would like to share with you that I believe people who are gay, lesbian, transgender, bisexual, or queer, are that way because that's how they were born. And more than that, they are even wired that way as a design by God. I believe that men and women who are attracted to the same sex are not doing so simply out of choice, but because that's who they are.

I believe that someone who identifies as LGBTQ can be just as much a fully committed follower of Jesus as you or I can. And I believe their love and commitment to God can be just as true as mine. And I believe that God's posture toward them is the same as toward me: a loving parent toward a child.

I believe that gay people who are in a loving and committed monogamous same-sex relationship are not sinning, and it is not a damnable offense. I believe these are people, humans like you and me, that deserve the right to love and be loved. And more so, because the LGBTQ are the most discriminated-against segment of our society, it is imperative that the church learn to open its doors and its hearts to embrace, love, and celebrate them as full participants in the Kingdom of God.

No Way Forward

"Who ordered the *carnitas* bowl?" Amanda asked, as she stepped into the narrow room adjacent to the Worship Center. You haven't experienced the full spectrum of what it means to be a pastor until you've sat in a room with tinted windows, designed for nursing mothers, eating Chipotle while waiting on a board to decide your fate.

Amanda was Sean's wife, and she must have arrived while I was in the meeting with the elders. She was there, like Sean, to be present and supportive of Kate and me. And she knew we would need to eat. Sometimes the simplest gestures—sitting next to someone or bringing food—are the best gifts to offer scared and hurting people.

The four of us, Sean, Amanda, Kate, and I, ate our lunches while going back and forth, talking about what just happened in the meeting and about random subjects as a distraction. There were only three rocking chairs, so I sat on the floor with my carnitas bowl (it was me; I ordered it) poking at the pasture-raised pig that gave his life so that I could try to not think about what was happening.

The meeting lasted eighty-one minutes. I know because I have the recording. The secretary of the board placed a small tape recorder on the table in the middle of the room to document the meeting. Since Kate couldn't be present, I asked him for a copy so that she could know what I had experienced. However, neither one of us listened to that recording until recently, while I was preparing to write this part of the story. I searched my archive, dropped the mp3 into iTunes, and settled in with a hot cup of coffee, unsure of what to expect.

It was a fascinating listen. I found myself proud of the Colby on that tape, who courageously spoke his beliefs in hostile territory, intent on being true to what was going on in his life. I was also sad at how the men in the room seemed so full of fear: Fear of new ideas. Fear of expanding theologies. Fear of how my situation might scare off donors and diminish church attendance.

I could also sense that everyone felt a degree of betrayal that morning.

I felt betrayed by men whom I'd loved and served for five years. I knew their children, their passions, their hopes and dreams. But all that mattered to them, in the end, was that I was a threat to their stability as an organization.

I think they felt betrayed that I wandered into liberal territory and jeopardized the church's momentum. At that time we were in the process of designing a brand-new, state-of-the-art, innovative worship facility. The church had outgrown its bland concrete box auditorium and was knee-deep in conversations with architects and strategizing for capital campaigns. But here I was, in their minds, constantly destabilizing progress by stirring up controversies on Facebook.

So when I listen to the recording of that fateful meeting now, I do so with compassion and grace, believing that we were all doing our best to live into our convictions. I could no longer remain in the closet about my theology, and they could no longer permit a pastor like me to remain on staff. It took about two years, but now I can say that I am not angry at them as people. My anger—or maybe frustration is a better word, or disappointment—is directed at the theological convictions that led them to a place where they felt that firing me was their only choice. I wasn't wounded by men; I was wounded by a weak gospel, a faulty narrative, a flimsy story of who they believe God is and how they understand humanity. Their belief system required them to protect the gates, lest their flock be led astray. And I was, to them, a wolf in skinny sheep jeans. How do I fault them for carrying out, with consistency, the logical conclusion of their convictions?

"So what did they say, after you finished reading your letter?" Kate asked, in between bites of rice and beans.

I had just told the three of them how I ended by saying,

> I realize that my positions place me outside the circle of Western conservative evangelicalism, which means it probably places me outside your circles as well, but I conclude by asking you to consider if maybe that's okay. Is this difference in theology something that is cause to break fellowship over? Is this cause to break ministry partnership over? Does this disqualify me from being a pastor here? And if so, then why? When Jesus didn't address it, why is this something to break fellowship over? I have never pushed a gay agenda or taught my views, and I have no plans to do either. I love you all.

I tried to think back.

"I remember Jonathan asking me how, in light of our significant disagreements on this issue, did I think we could continue doing ministry together."

"How'd you respond?" Sean asked.

"I pointed out that we had been doing just that, over these past five years, working together in spite of our differences. I named the many beliefs we held in common, and the shared values we had for doing church together and chasing after the Kingdom. I suggested we view this for what it is: a secondary theological issue that has not historically been an essential doctrine of the Christian faith."

Today, where I am in life, I disagree with that Colby. While it's true that homosexuality has never been an essential doctrine of the faith, I think it's impractical—if not detrimental—for pastors of the same church to be on such extreme sides of the fence when it comes to the question of the sinfulness of homosexuality. Members of the LGBTQ community, who are looking for a safe and sacred place to worship and to practice their Christianity, need to know that the men and women shepherding them are not hiding disgust toward same-sex relationships. They need to know, with clarity and certainty, whether or not they will be honored and celebrated as equal members of the body of Christ. They deserve honesty with where their leaders stand so as not to fall victim to a spirit-crushing bait-and-switch. I have seen the devastation firsthand when LGBTQ Christians invest in a faith community, only to feel blindsided when they discover the truth: their non-affirming pastor, disguised as loving and welcoming toward all people, actually expects them to either remain celibate or undergo some sort of doomed-to-fail attempt at conversion therapy. But even more important, because sexuality has become the proverbial line in the sand, I think gay-affirming pastors need to come out of the theological closet sooner rather than later. We need you out here. There is so much work to be done to mend the damage the church has caused. The cultural tide has shifted, and, praise God, young girls and boys are growing up in a world that is more and more accepting of who they are. Now we just need churches, and church leaders, who can meet them outside the sanctuary doors and say, "God loves you just the way you are. Come, the Table is set, but it's not complete without you."

But I can understand the Colby I hear in the recording of that meeting; the Colby who still hoped, on some level, to remain in Arizona but who also knew that he could no longer do it while remaining in the closet about his views. My capacity for being out of alignment had been reached. So I was trying to suggest a way forward: where I could remain employed in the midst of the tension. Where I could pursue wholeness between my convictions and my actions but also serve alongside and underneath leadership that vehemently disagreed with me.

I'm grateful they didn't think my plan was a good one.

When Fear Wins

"We need to take the weekend to think things over and pray about this," Frank said, as he and Jonathan called me back into the office. The board deliberated for about half an hour after our meeting, and I have no idea what they talked about, but now everyone was gone except for Frank and Jonathan. "In the meantime, don't worry about leading worship on Sunday. We have made plans accordingly. Just take the weekend off."

Twice, in high school, I was benched by my basketball coach. Each time was because I had made a costly mistake that lost us a game. So either because the coach had lost faith in me or because he wanted to teach me a lesson, I didn't start the following game. It crushed me both times. But compared to getting yanked from the platform where I'd led worship for five years straight, those moments barely register. It made me feel like a criminal, a deviant sinner from whom the board had to protect the vulnerable flock.

Kate and I left the church and went home to be with our boys, numb and unsure how it would all play out. Over that weekend, the situation got even more tense and messy as speculation increased about what was happening with me. I wasn't permitted to disclose much, which made it hard to answer the few people who reached out to us. The grapevine also delivered occasional messages about some of what was being said about me, and it hurt. To be fair, there probably is no such thing as a "good way to fire people." It's clunky and confusing, and when you add the dimension of being a church it's guaranteed to be painful.

Sunday came and went. Kate and I visited another church that morning, and in the evening we stopped by Jonathan's house to check in with what was happening.

"Tuesday morning," he said. "Come on in, and we'll talk."

I reflected on the previous week: Tuesday—the president repealed Don't Ask Don't Tell, and I voiced my support on Facebook. Wednesday—I took the post down in response to "concern." Thursday—I wrote a ten-page letter to the board articulating my stance on homosexuality. Friday—I came out of the theological closet. Saturday—I juggled rumors and misconceptions. Sunday—I wasn't allowed to lead my faith community in worship, which I had no idea would come to mean that I'd never see them again. Monday was a day off, and then Tuesday I drove to the church, where I was told I would be presented with a plan permitting me to remain employed—involving probation, a public apology, and education designed to help set me straight.

But the air was all wrong when I showed up at Jonathan's office and took my place in the same chair where I had sat just three days prior. I thought back to the nerves I endured at the district office, in the room with high ceilings and floral patterns, waiting for Ruth to ask her question. I recalled my longing for a group of people to look at me and say, "That guy, right there, we deem him fit to be a pastor," and the pride and relief that came when they did just that. Call me naive, but I don't think I ever considered the possibility that another group of people, in a different room, would come along, later down the road, and reverse that affirmation.

"Thanks for coming in today, Colby," Jonathan began. "This isn't easy for any of us, and I'm truly sorry that it's come to this." He reached across the coffee table and handed me a single piece of paper.

Effective immediately, my service at the church was no longer needed.

Sure, I was now out of the theological closet. And yes, I had at last found a path toward aligning my internal convictions with my external reality. But the first few steps, it turned out, would lead me free-falling into unemployment and disillusionment.

He who wants to find his life first must lose it.

Consider it lost.

CHAPTER 6

———————————→

REDEFINING THE BOUNDARIES

Leviticus 18:22 and 20:13

The hard metal chair threatened to tip forward as I leaned in closer to catch every lyric. Inside the cold banquet room above the dining hall, I heard Andrew Peterson for the first time when he played a concert at my college. I'm certain he had no idea that his words would crack open a chamber of my heart that previously lay dormant. The opening lines of his song "Come, Lord Jesus" bore into my consciousness that evening and planted seeds of compassion in the newly opened section of my heart, most notably when he sang about perusing magazine covers while standing in line at a grocery store, "I saw the pictures of the prophets with the picket signs, / Screaming 'God hates fags!'"[1]

At eighteen years old, as a freshman in college, this was the first time I can remember being confronted with the reality of so-called Christians holding picket signs of condemnation toward the LGBTQ community.[2] It was so unsettling. I couldn't shake the image for the rest of the night. I was wrecked with thoughts like, *even if God is against homosexuality, how in the world can anyone who professes to follow Christ say that God hates that person?* This led me to other questions regarding where people got the idea in the first place that a gay person is something to be despised, loathed, feared, treated like a criminal, and cast to the fringes of society.

As I would come to find out, the source for such indignation came from a place where the cynics smirk unsurprised, and the naive are left bewildered: the Bible.

It Is an Abomination

The second and third passages I'm setting out to UnClobber are also from the Old Testament. They're both found in the book of Leviticus, and they have armed fundamentalists with the language of vitriol.

> You shall not lie with a male as with a woman; it is an abomination. (Lev. 18:22 ESV)

> If a man lies with a male as with a woman, both of them have committed an abomination; they shall surely be put to death; their blood is upon them. (Lev. 20:13 ESV)

The catchphrase "homosexuality is an abomination" has reverberated out of bullhorns on countless street corners, filled more than its share of picket signs, and ended many online discussion threads. *Abomination* is a loaded word, evoking something subhuman, vile, and gross.[3] And while I'm certain that most Christians (the aforementioned picketers notwithstanding) would never intend to communicate that a gay person is vile or subhuman, the reality is that this happens every day in subtle ways. It is a natural outcome of the belief that people who are attracted to the same gender or who are in same-sex relationships are an abomination.

In his book *Unclean*, Richard Beck talks about "infrahumanization," which is the phenomenon of seeing people as less than human. It happens when a group of people (usually those in power or in the majority) come to believe another group of people does not possess some vital quality or characteristic that defines what it means to be human. In particular, this can be done through denying secondary emotions to these out-group members. Secondary emotions (such as love, hope, admiration, pride, conceit, nostalgia, and remorse) are quintessential *human* emotions, in contrast with the primary emotions (pain, pleasure, fear, joy, surprise, and anger) we share with the animal world. To suggest, then, that a person or a group of people does not or cannot exhibit a particular secondary emotion—whether suggested implicitly or explicitly—is, in short, to see them as less than human.[4]

Tragically, I see this process of infrahumanization occur within the in-group of heterosexuals toward those in the LGBTQ community, not least of all in the church. If you have ever heard a statement such as, "Gay people cannot control themselves sexually or stay in a monogamous relationship," or "The gay community is pushing their gay agenda down our throats," then you can understand what I'm talking about. These sorts of statements attack the gay community's capacity for secondary emotions (i.e., love, fidelity, sincerity). By way of example, consider how slaveholders in the American South denied that African Americans could feel and experience emotions in the same way that white folks could, allowing for the disastrous dehumanization of black people.

Once a person, or a group of people, has been infrahumanized, he or she has, for all intents and purposes, become a monster. And monsters do not deserve to be treated with kindness, respect, or compassion. This, I argue, is what has happened (and is happening) as a result of some

Christians' insistence that "homosexuality is an abomination." It dehumanizes gay people, which then allows us to treat them horribly[5] without conflict of conscience because they are "not like us."

I'm not suggesting that your average Christian does this intentionally. To be fair, not everyone who says, "homosexuality is an abomination," would then turn and say, "gay people are monsters." But the failure to see how the one attitude inevitably leads to the other is part of the root problem of this systemic discriminatory posture toward the LGBTQ community.

My hope, then, is to explore the two Clobber Passages in Leviticus and see if we can grasp what it meant back then for an act to be considered an "abomination." And why would that have been the case? And how are we to understand these verses today in the twenty-first century? Are they indeed biblical imperatives that the church should still be holding up?

I believe the church has misused these texts to speak a dehumanizing word over and against our LGBTQ siblings. As you'll see, these Clobber Passages do not add helpful substance to the conversation around what we now understand about sexual orientation; nor do they offer an authoritative word against those involved in a loving, committed, mutually respecting same-sex relationship.

But first, here's an introductory word about the book of Leviticus.

A New Way for a New People

After more than four hundred years as brick-making slaves in Egypt, God (through Moses, Aaron, and the oft-ignored Miriam) liberated the Hebrew people, freeing them to become their own nation. Israel, now wandering the wilderness in search of the promised land, was left with the existential question, "If we are not slave people, owned by others and whose worth is measured on how many bricks we make, then who are we?" They would soon learn that they were to become the people-group through whom God would reveal to the world more and more of who God is.

Leviticus, then, is a collection of commandments and laws compiled for the priestly tribe (the Levites) who were responsible for the religious aspects of the community. The book can be broken down into three main sections: The Sacrificial Cult (chapters 1–10), Ritual Pollution and Purification (chapters 11–17), and the Holiness Code (chapters 18–27). The first two sections outline how the Hebrews ought to function religiously toward God, while the third section (where the Clobber Passages are found) is about how they ought to function toward one another.

At a fundamental level, the people of Israel were called to live unlike every other nation around them. God was doing a new thing, and Leviticus (along with Deuteronomy and Numbers) chronicled Israel's early years of figuring out what that looked like.

So as you read through Leviticus, it's important to keep in mind that, although some (many?) of the prohibitions seem strange to us now, back then these commands were ripe with meaning. Not only that, they were intentionally designed to showcase a new way of being and doing in the world—a new way to understand humanity, God, and the relationships between them. This is summarized in the opening verses of chapter 18, the beginning of the Holiness Code section:

> And the LORD spoke to Moses, saying, "Speak to the people of Israel and say to them, I am the LORD your God. You shall not do as they do in the land of Egypt, where you lived, and you shall not do as they do in the land of Canaan, to which I am bringing you. You shall not walk in their statutes. You shall follow my rules and keep my statutes and walk in them. I am the LORD your God. (vv. 1–4 ESV)

God said, "Do not do as they do in Egypt, where you came from . . . and do not do as they do in Canaan, where I'm taking you." Israel's calling was to be different, to be *holy* (meaning "set apart"). Some commands appear to us to be issues of morality, whereas other commands seem rather arbitrary and even amoral. But all of them were designed to be a new way for a new people.

Violations against the Family

Let's take a quick tour through the broader context of our first Clobber Passage, found in Leviticus 18.

The primary focus of chapter 18 is on prohibitions against violating the family dynamic, not least of all through incest. Committing any of these acts is considered an "abomination" (18:26 ESV), a word we'll come back to later on.

After the introduction (quoted above), verse 6 (ESV) says, "None of you shall approach any one of his close relatives to uncover nakedness," and what follows are fourteen more verses laying out every conceivable possibility for incest: no sex with your aunts, uncles, your siblings, your mother or stepmother. You name it, it's off limits.

Then verse 21 seems to take a detour when it prohibits sacrificing your child to the Canaanite god Molech, but it's reasonable to assume that would have been an affront to the sacredness of family as well. And then we arrive at our Clobber Passage, in verse 22, "You shall not lie with a male as with a woman; *it is an abomination*" (ESV, emphasis mine). The section then wraps up with a prohibition against bestiality in verse 23.

The chapter ends with God saying that all these activities were engaged in by the people God was currently evicting from the promised land. God said, "But you shall keep my statutes and my ordinances and commit none of these abominations [meaning, *all* the behaviors previously listed in the chapter]. . . . So keep my charge not to commit any of these abominable customs that were practiced before you, and never to make yourselves unclean by them: I am the LORD your God" (Lev. 18:26, 30 ESV).

We have eighteen verses designed to protect the family dynamic, the family ethos, and the sacredness of the family. Eighteen verses are filled with prohibitions against sexual relations with people in your family, against child sacrifice, against men lying with men, and against sex with animals.

All these things the Egyptians did. All these things the Canaanites did. Now Israel was being called to something different, something new, something better.

I think we can get tripped up sometimes when we think of the Law as some arbitrary set of rules, as though God is beholden to some greater cosmic document that outlines what is "right" and what is "wrong." But these laws were not (and are not) arbitrary; they have a purpose. As Jesus would one day say, "'You shall love the Lord your God with all your heart and with all your soul and with all your mind. This is the great and first commandment. And a second is like it: You shall love your neighbor as yourself. On these two commandments depend all the Law and the Prophets" (Matt. 22:37–40 ESV). Paul would later affirm, "For the whole law is fulfilled in one word: 'You shall love your neighbor as yourself'" (Gal. 5:14 ESV). The Law was designed to move people toward love of God, self, and neighbor. Therefore, any attempt to understand the laws today (and understand how we might attempt to apply them today, if at all) must be done within the context of moving people toward love.

Now then, let's unpack the prohibition found in Leviticus 18:22.

More Confusion than Clarity

Once we realize that the story of Sodom and Gomorrah was not about the inherent sinfulness of same-sex attraction, nor was it intended to be a cosmic declaration that any and all same-sex sex acts are an offense to God, then all we are left with—in terms of an Old Testament prohibition against homosexuality—are these two verses in Leviticus. If it's true, then, that these two Clobber Passages were specifically intended to warn ancient Israel about the dangers and sinfulness of same-sex relations, then we wouldn't be crazy for expecting clarity and certainty. A lot is at stake, after all.

But before we look closer at the word *abomination*, I want to make a couple of observations about what we find in the original Hebrew language in Leviticus 18:22 and 20:13 (phrased identically until 20:13 mentions a death penalty). I know that talking about ancient languages is not everyone's idea of a good time, but I hope you'll stick with me because an exploration of the Hebrew leaves me feeling anything but certain and clear.

First, there is an odd juxtaposition of nouns. In Hebrew there is one word for "man/husband" *(ish)* and a different word for "males" in general *(zakar)*. And the same goes for women: a particular word for "woman/wife" *(ishsha)* and a different word for "females" *(neqevah)*. Typically, you expect them to be used together: "man/husband with woman/wife" *(ish* with *ishsha)* or "male with female" *(zakar* with *neqevah)*. However, in these verses, the lawgiver uses the general "male" *(zakar)* but then switches to the particular "woman/wife" *(ishsha)*. If indeed the prohibition was intended to cover any and all instances of men having sex with men, we would expect a more general, "You shall not lie with males *(zakar)* as you lie with females *(neqevah)*." Or it might be even more specific: "You shall not lie with a man/husband *(ish)* as you do a woman/wife *(ishsha)*." But the Hebrew says, "You shall not lie with *mankind* as you do with a *woman/wife*." This suggests a nuanced or situational prohibition, as opposed to an across-the-board law against any and all sex acts between men.

Second, if these verses were meant to prohibit homosexual relations, then the second half of the verses become superfluous. In other words, if the law was intended to universally prohibit men having sex with men, then why have the phrase "as with a woman/wife" at all? Again, I think this points to a more specific or nuanced context. This becomes more intriguing when considering that, according to a Jewish hermeneutical principle (that is, a framework for interpreting the Bible), when a generalization is followed by a specification, only what is specified applies.[6] Apply that principle here, and the generalization ("you shall not lie with a male") is there only to highlight the specific ("as with a woman/wife"). Meaning, the Levitical lawmaker is referring to one particular expression of men laying with males. This is different than a sweeping condemnation against any and all same-sex sex acts between men.

Also interesting is the uncertainty with which translators handle the Hebrew phrase *mishkevey ishsha*, which over time became the lackadaisical English translation "as with a woman." We've already covered *ishsha* (woman/wife); that's the easy part. (Although the question still remains: did the Levitical lawgiver intend the reader to think "woman" or "wife?" And might it change the application either way?) But combining it with the other word, *mishkevey*, is when it gets curious. *Mishkevey* is the plural form of *mishkab*, which means "bed"; it was used as a euphemism for the "act of lying down for sexual contact." So, if we attempt a literal translation, it would be, "the layings of a woman" or "the beds of a wife." The only other time this curious word *mishkevey* is used is in Genesis 49:4, when Jacob has harsh words for his son Reuben who, in Genesis 35, slept with one of his father's concubines and defiled his *mishkevey* (place of layings). However, *mishkevey ishsha* is a strange and unique combination of words that is used nowhere else, and so scholars have had to do some guesswork to figure out what the lawmaker was saying. When attempting to translate this phrase to English, beginning in 1530 with William Tyndale, translators inserted the not-in-the-original-Hebrew prepositional phrase "as with." Which says to me that translating the Hebrew to say, "You shall not lie with mankind *as with* a woman/wife," was less about a direct translation, and more about filling in the vague Hebrew with an English preposition to support a particular interpretation.[7]

The final observation I wish to make is what *isn't* there — namely, any word against lesbianism. Even the most ardent supporters of the traditional perspective acknowledge the Bible's lack of words against female same-sex sex acts (with the possible exception of Romans 1:26, which we'll get to in chapter 8). If we accept that these two Clobber Passages were inserted in to Israel's Holiness Code book for the purpose of informing humanity about the divine prohibition against homosexuality, then why are female same-sex sex acts never addressed? That omission cannot be overstated.[8]

These four observations raise legitimate questions about the Old Testament's clarity on the inherent sinfulness of homosexuality, and on any and all same-sex sex acts. There is no doubt that the lawmaker was prohibiting some sort of male-male sex act, but there is doubt as to the exact nature of the prohibition. The clunky Hebrew idioms — that we don't fully understand — combined with the unexpected juxtaposition of nouns and the lack of prepositions connecting everything as we'd expect, ought to slow down a person before she or he quotes Leviticus as a definitive biblical word against homosexuality. These ambiguities and uncertainties in the text make for shaky ground on which to stake a claim that God clearly prohibits homosexuality in the Old Testament.

And even *if* these Clobber Passages could adequately cover any and all same-sex sex acts between men (which I don't think they do), they still do not offer any word regarding homosexuality as an orientation, nor do they address sex acts between two women.

Transgressing the Boundary

Let's move from the clunky and confusing parts of these Clobber Passages to the more easily interpreted—yet still misunderstood—parts: the word *abomination*.

It comes from the Hebrew word *toevah*. This is a plural noun which, in short, was used to stipulate certain actions that, if committed, would render an Israelite indistinguishable from the surrounding nations, a betrayal of the Lord's unique calling to live holy (aka, set apart). *Toevah* were cultural taboos, if you will. They transgressed the boundary that was supposed to delineate the Israelite people from both the Egyptians (from whence they came) and the Canaanites (to where they were going). Here is how *toevah* is unpacked in Deuteronomy 18:9–12:

> When you come into the land that the LORD your God is giving you, you shall not learn to follow the abominable practices [*toevah*] of those nations. There shall not be found among you anyone who burns his son or his daughter as an offering, anyone who practices divination or tells fortunes or interprets omens, or a sorcerer or a charmer or a medium or a necromancer or one who inquires of the dead, for whoever does these things is an abomination [*toevah*] to the LORD. (ESV)

The importance of grasping what it meant for an object, action, or person to be called a *toevah* cannot be overstated. Therefore, I want to survey some of the other usages in the Old Testament that illustrate how *toevah* was used. I'll make three observations: (1) *toevah* was relative in nature, (2) it was not synonymous with "sinful," and (3) it was used to describe the improper mixing of substances and/or the transgressing of boundaries.

First, a word about the relative nature of *toevah*. Calling actions *toevah* implied violation of cultural divisions.

They were actions that caused the boundaries between people groups to disappear. Other cultures had their own set of behaviors considered *toevah*. For example, in Genesis 43, Joseph's brothers met up with him in Egypt and shared a meal together, but the Egyptians did not eat with them because it was "[*toevah*] to the Egyptians" to eat with Hebrews (Gen. 43:32 ESV). Not only that; shepherds in general were considered *toevah* to the Egyptians (see Gen. 46:34). But the best example comes from Exodus 8 when Moses requested that Pharaoh allow the Hebrew people to offer sacrifices to their God outside the Egyptian borders. His reasoning was, "It would not be right to do so, for the offerings we shall sacrifice to the LORD our God are [*toevah*] an abomination to the Egyptians" (Exod. 8:26 ESV).

In other words, innocuous actions such as being a shepherd or eating with Hebrew people, and (at least from the perspective of the Old Testament) virtuous actions such as the sacrifices of the Hebrew people, were called offensive—an abomination, *toevah*—by the Egyptian people. This should be enough for us to question the loaded translation of "abomination" for *toevah*, which suggests (as mentioned above) actions that are vile, gross, or subhuman—words we would not use to describe the sacred acts of sacrificial worship that Moses and his people wanted to make to Yahweh. No, *toevah* had a relative nature, which leads to the second observation.

If an act was identified as *toevah*, it did not therefore mean that the act in question was inherently, objectively, or eternally an immoral offense or a violation of God's will. In other words, *toevah* was not synonymous with sinful. But that is the sense we get with the word *abomination*. There were other words in the Hebrew language the lawgiver could have used to describe the prohibitions in Leviticus 18 as sinful or immoral, but he didn't. He used *toevah*. This is not to suggest, of course, that there couldn't also be a sense in which some (or possibly all) of the prohibitions listed were seen as immoral. For instance, no one will argue for a relative approach to sacrificing children or argue that it's not an evil and immoral act.

My point is that if an object or action was identified as *toevah*, then that is not, in and of itself, a sufficient reason for us in the twenty-first century to definitively declare that same activity, if committed today, as a sinful, immoral, objective offense. Just because an action is labeled *toevah* doesn't mean that the action belongs in the category of "always a sin in the eyes of the Lord." For example, in Deuteronomy 25, we find a list of instructions regarding how to handle certain controversies and conflicts between Israelites, such as not delivering more than forty lashes on a condemned offender (v. 3) or not muzzling an ox that treads the corn (v. 4), and the importance of a man marrying his brother's wife if his brother dies (vv. 5–10). Then, in one of the Bible's most fantastic verses (vv. 11–12), the Israelite people were instructed to cut off the hand of a woman if, while her husband is in a fight with another man, she attempts to aid her husband by grabbing the testicles of the other man (as the KJV puts it, "taketh him by the secrets"). The chapter then ends with an admonition to use proper weights when measuring goods so as to not rob one another (vv. 13–15). After all these instructions are laid out, we read, "For all who do such things, all who act dishonestly, are an abomination [*toevah*] to the LORD your God" (v. 16 ESV).

While we might try and understand why some of those actions were seen as *toevah* back in ancient Israel and while we could probably identify the heart behind some of these instructions, the fact remains that no reasonable Christian today would look at that list in Deuteronomy 25 and say that all those actions are inherently and eternally a sin against God. Rather, they were illustrative of the ways that the surrounding nations conducted themselves, and therefore they should not be descriptive of Israel's way of life.

To further make the point about both the relative and the not-synonymous-with-sinful nature of *toevah*, consider

Deuteronomy 14:1–21. Once again *toevah* is used to separate what might be acceptable for other nations but is forbidden for Israel. Verse 3 says, "You shall not eat *toevah*," followed by a long list of which animals are clean and good to eat, and which ones are not. The passage culminates with, "You shall not eat anything that has died naturally. You may give it to the sojourner who is within your towns, that he may eat it, or you may sell it to a foreigner. For you are a people holy [set apart] to the LORD your God" (v. 21 ESV). Notice that what is forbidden for Israel is not forbidden for the person passing through their lands. If *toevah* was intended to communicate "that which is always evil and offensive to God," then why were they encouraged to give *toevah* items to non-Israelites?

The answer is because *toevah* was not about morality. It was about identity. It was about violating the cultural boundary markers that preserved the holiness, the set-apartness, of this emerging people group of freed slaves. Deuteronomy also explained the importance of eradicating the people in the cities they were going to conquer, lest any survivors "teach you to do according to all their [*toevah*] abominable practices that they have done for their gods" (Deut. 20:18 ESV). Yet, as you read about the decline of morality among the kings and the Israelites as recorded in the books of 1 and 2 Kings and 1 and 2 Chronicles, you hear how the historians would look back through time at Israel's history, reflecting on how everything went wrong and resulted in the Jewish people being sent into exile and blamed it on the people committing the "[*toevah*] of the nations which the LORD cast out before the children of Israel" (1 Kgs. 14:24 KJV).[9]

My final observation about *toevah* has to do with how the word was used to describe improper mixing, beyond the transgression of cultural practices. In Deuteronomy 22, for instance, we read about the *toevah* of mixing outfits, aka, cross dressing (22:5), mixing types of seeds planted in the ground (22:9), and mixing wool and linen together to make clothing (22:11). All of this supports the idea that *toevah* is rooted not in evil or immoral actions but in a particular refusal to combine and mix things that should not be mixed. Israel was to be set apart, and *toevah* behaviors threatened the entire project. They described activities that transgressed the boundary markers of what it meant to be Israel. They did not describe activities that were inherently wicked, even if it's true that some *toevah* would have also been seen as such.

Understanding Abomination, Then and Now

Summarizing our unpacking of these two Clobber Passages, it's still unclear precisely who the prohibitions were aimed at and what exact activities were off limits. Some scholars maintain that Leviticus applied *only* to men of the priestly tribe of Levi. Other scholars maintain that these Clobber Passages applied *only* to Jewish men living in the Holy Land.[10] And did they only apply within the context of the family? What is to be said about the lack of any condemnation toward women, if indeed this was intended to be a divine word against any and all same-sex sex acts?

Furthermore, with a better understanding of what it meant for something to be *toevah*, even if we succeeded in identifying what was being prohibited in the Clobber Passages, we must still acknowledge the primary motivation behind why it was prohibited in the first place: because it was a violation of cultural boundaries, *not* because it was evil or unnatural. So while we can say with certainty that under Levitical Law a man "shall not lie with a male as with a woman" (whatever specific activity that might have meant) because it blurred the lines of the Israelites with the Egyptians and Canaanites, we cannot say with certainty whether or not a man lying with a male as with a woman was evil or sinful. That is simply beyond the scope of what it meant for something to be *toevah*.

Yet, because our English translations use the word *abomination* to describe a man "laying with a male the layings of a woman/wife," any expression today of same-sex intimacy gets linked to adjectives like vile, gross, and subhuman. The word *abomination* is loaded with meaning and implications that add an interpretive layer to *toevah* and takes it places where it was never meant to go.

When we take into account the way *toevah* was used in ancient Israel, then I can't imagine a scenario where it makes sense to apply these laws to us today. Especially if we consider how Jesus redefined what it means to be in relationship with God. The Hebrew people, as part of the family of God, were given the Law as a way to live out their calling. Under the teachings, life, death, and resurrection of Jesus, however, we have been given a new way to live out our calling: faith. And we have been given a new way to understand the purpose and fulfillment of the entirety of the Law: Love God and love your neighbor as yourself.

So how do specific laws about not transgressing the boundary between Israel and other cultures speak to our world today? I'm not convinced they can.

This brings us back to the question: what do these two Clobber Passages have to say about homosexuality as an orientation or with regard to a loving, committed, same-sex relationship? I cannot, in good conscience (or in good scholarship), see how these two verses, which were written to help a liberated group of slaves understand how they were to be a uniquely called-out nation in the world, can offer any words of condemnation against the LGBTQ community.

These two Clobber Passages have been misused for too long to condemn the LGBTQ community and make them feel that they are less than human. That is not only wrong morally, it is also wrong biblically.

It's Time to ReHumanize

After teaching on these two Clobber Passages one evening several years ago, a man came up to me and said, "I hear what you're saying, but isn't it still true that, as a gay man, it would have been awful for me back in ancient Israel? Wouldn't I still have been denied any attempt to live out my innate attraction to other men? Even if you are successful in UnClobbering these passages for today, I still would not have been affirmed and accepted in ancient Israel, would I?"

I could see the desperation in his eyes, wanting to find validation for who he is and feeling scared that any sort of word against him thirty-five hundred years ago would still count as a word against him today.

"No, you're right, you would not have been affirmed or celebrated, and you would not have been permitted to openly enjoy a relationship with another man. So yes, life would have been awful if you tried. You could get killed for it. That being said, though, recall that the same arguments could be made for being a woman in the ancient world. It would have been awful in many ways to be a woman—or a child, for that matter. A rebellious child also could have been killed. The ancient patriarchal world was brutal, and many of its laws were founded on assumptions about the superiority of men. Sure, Levitical Law did much to help humanity move forward in terms of raising human consciousness and creating a more just and generous world, but we had a long way to go. And we still do. You are correct; life would have been hard for you. But you wouldn't have been the only one. And so thank God you are alive now, in this day, and can step into your calling to be a beloved child of God!"

I'm not sure how much my words helped, but I hope he understood my point. I guess what I'm saying is, based on what I've argued in this chapter, we need to stop using ancient Levitical Laws that were designed for a specific purpose and a specific people as a means for understanding who we are today. It is not the proper place to discover what God's dream is for us today and what it might look like to engage in a loving, committed, mutually respecting relationship with another person.

When it comes to questioning the sinfulness of people born with same-sex attraction, or the sinfulness of a gay couple living together in a loving, committed relationship, these two verses in Leviticus simply do not help.

They are not trying to answer those questions.

And they do not provide cause for a belief that our gay and lesbian friends and family members are vile, gross, or subhuman.

It's time we close down the online message boards, throw away the picket signs, and shut up the bullhorns on the street corner, because those are the things that are truly abominable.

CHAPTER 7

———————————→

IN SEARCH OF THE UNICORN

Progressive and Christian

No one goes to the dentist because they like it: sitting in that oversized chair under that obnoxiously bright light, with your mouth pried open, sharp tools jamming your gums. We go because, as unpleasant as the process is, we know it's important for our long-term well-being.

After coming out of the theological closet and subsequently getting fired, I was more aligned than I'd ever been before. Naively I expected to feel—if not great—then at least relief. Finally I could go to bed at night knowing that I didn't have to hide any longer. However, even though my life on the outside could now begin reflecting my beliefs on the inside, the good feelings I expected to accompany the shift toward wholeness would be months away from manifesting. Instead, the next few weeks felt like being strapped to a dentist chair, and I had to keep reminding myself that, as painful as it was, this was the best chance I had for long-term health.

The days following my termination were demoralizing as I struggled to see what options I had. Should I go *back* in the theological closet, dust off my résumé, and get another gig as a worship pastor in the evangelical world I knew so well? Or stay on my new theological path and become—what—an Episcopal priest? While I knew they would accept my thoughts on homosexuality and the Bible, their liturgical style of doing church (while at times a welcome reprieve) doesn't resonate at my deepest levels. Neither option appealed to me. There were days when I wondered if being a closeted pastor in an ill-fitting environment was still better than not being a pastor at all.

The idea that a church existed that was oriented around Jesus and the Kingdom, had the vibe and feel of the evangelical world I was used to (i.e., guitars and drums in worship), and was also progressive in its theology felt as elusive and mythical as a unicorn.

What was I to do? Where was I to go? Was this a sign that I was not meant to be a pastor? And how could a church reject one of their own this way? What does that say about faith communities? What does that say about God?

So many questions . . . so few answers.

Little did I know that the secret to finding the unicorn is to stay still, pay attention, and let it come to you.[1]

You Should Connect With . . .

Two days after I was fired, I met my friend Brian for coffee. He was the worship pastor at a nearby church and one of the few people I'd made a meaningful connection with outside my own congregation. Before we said our good-byes, he told me about a friend of his who was an openly gay pastor at a church in San Diego. "Maybe you'd want to connect with him," Brian offered, as we left the coffee shop in downtown Chandler. I thanked him for the thought and mentally cataloged the data.

Two days later, my friend Talitha sent me an email to express her condolences. She worked at a non-profit in San Diego and mentioned a guy she knew named Todd. Todd was also openly gay and happened to be the lead pastor at the *exact same church* in San Diego! "Maybe you'd want to connect with him," Talitha suggested.

Two friends, from two different social circles, within two days of each other, told me about two openly gay pastors from the same church!

I couldn't *not* follow this up.

After we exchanged a few emails, Todd offered to cover our costs if we wanted to drive over to San Diego and attend a conference they were hosting, where he said we would get the chance to connect with other progressive Christians. We jumped at the opportunity to get out of Arizona for a few days and enjoy a free trip to our favorite city. While we were at that conference, I let myself believe that maybe, *just maybe,* there might be churches out there for someone like me.

But before we made it over to San Diego for the conference, we first had to weather more storms from the fallout of my firing.

Support in Unlikely Places

If he was surprised by my profanity-laced tirade or by my golf bag being hurled across the parking lot, he didn't show it.

Kyle, my friend since high school, flew down to Arizona just days after I was fired, for no other reason than to take me golfing, drink craft beer, and give Kate and me a much-needed reminder that we still had friends. In the weeks that followed my termination, we were crushed by the lack of care and support we received from many of our former church friends. However, there was a community of people outside our church that gave us significant kindness, empathy, and support. In a tragic twist of irony, the wave of emotional support that came from this outside community would end up threatening our only source of financial support: my severance package. I was golfing with Kyle when I received the voice mail that put our livelihood in jeopardy.

But let me back up for a moment.

When I got home from clearing out my desk, one of the first decisions Kate and I made was to prayerfully consider what the path of peace would look like. As tempting as it was to log onto Facebook, tap out a tweet, and post a new blog detailing the accounts of how I was fired from an evangelical megachurch over my theology on sexuality, our spirits told us that was not peacemaking behavior. So we chose not to put our story out there, not to reach out to people to tell them what happened, and not make any moves that might stir up trouble. For us, the path of peace meant that we would tell people what had happened only if they reached out to us first. And, considering how we ministered there for five years, it was disheartening how few did. Most people took the church's messaging and assumed that was that. *If they fired Colby*, they must have thought, *I'm sure it was the right decision. No need to ask questions.*

The letter that went out to the members of the church and the statement shared from the pulpit was light on details. "Because of Colby's theological positions," it read, "on issues that our leaders believe are central to Scripture and a life after God . . . we feel it is time to bring his time of service to an end." Before their letter went out, I gave them my blessing to say what the theological position was, but they didn't take me up on it. Don't Ask, Don't Tell was back on, it would seem.[2]

It was lonely for those first few days and weeks after I was fired. A handful of friends reached out with love and support, and were it not for them, I'm not sure we would have ever darkened the doors of another church. But in the face of so much pain and rejection, the numerically small group of friends who showed up for us felt like using a cocktail umbrella during a hail storm. So when an opportunity came along to share our story with a larger audience of people who could commiserate with us, but still be done in a way that would honor our desire to walk the path of peace, we jumped at the prospect to feel seen and understood.

There was a blogger in Southern California whom Kate and I, dreading our foreseeable loneliness, found as we feverishly Googled "open and affirming Christians." This blogger had been a vocal LGBTQ Christian activist for several years, so when I reached out to share my story with him two weeks after I was fired, I knew he would be a safe person to confide in. When he responded with empathetic indignation, I wept at feeling seen. One of the most powerful balms is hearing words like, "me too," and "you're not crazy."

He asked how I would feel if he shared my story with his readers, knowing that it would provide us with a deluge of love and encouragement. I talked it over with Kate, weighing the pros and the cons, and we decided to go for it. After all, the chances were nil that anyone at our former church followed or read his blog. But because of our commitment to the path of peace, I made one request: redact every name and detail that could in any way reveal my name or the name of the church. I was fine sharing my story with a handful of like-minded readers, but I had no desire to slander my former congregation and its people.

The redacting, however, was not as effective as I'd hoped.

His post went live on October 13, 2011. Now, compared to a Jimmy Fallon lip-synch battle or a Jon Stewart takedown of the GOP, the story didn't go viral. But with the headline "Pastor Fired for Linking to *Don't Ask, Don't Tell* Article," it definitely garnered attention within certain circles.[3] At the time it went live, I had just hit my drive off the first tee, confident that a round of golf and a couple beers with Kyle would make another day in the dentist chair a little more tolerable. Throughout the round,

I kept refreshing my phone as the comments on the blog post poured in. Like-minded people from around the world both showered us with support and expressed outrage at the church that fired me. Kate and I texted back and forth, amazed at what people were saying.

Slowly the cocktail umbrella expanded, as people's words brought relief and solidarity.

The encouragement and support we lacked from those we considered friends in real life, as it turned out, we would find anonymously through an online community of progressive Christians. Some of them even sent money because they knew we had three kids and another on the way. The love poured through their comments, restoring my soul like an embrace from your three-year-old after being gone for too long.

But the positivity was short-lived, not even lasting an entire round of golf.

I had just sat down in the golf cart, after tapping in my par putt on the eighteenth hole, when I saw the new voice mail red bubble. I tapped "play," held the phone to my ear, and listened. Stunned.

It was the church. Somehow they had gotten hold of the blog post, and it spread throughout the staff and larger church community. Though I said nothing disparaging about my former church, the narrative flowing through the rumor mill was that I trashed them online—which I hadn't, of course. But perception can be stronger than reality. They had worked hard to intentionally *not* let word out regarding the theological issue over which I was fired. But if people started passing the post around and linking it back to me, then the cat would never be back in the bag.

The voice mail essentially said, "We know what you did, and there will be consequences."

"Colby, are you okay?" Kyle inquired, as I set the phone down. I told him what the message was, but I played it cool. Shock, I think they call it. It wasn't until we drove the cart back toward my car that the gravity of the situation began to settle in.

Had I, through my desire to feel less alone and less crazy, jeopardized the well-being of my family? Did anonymously publishing my redacted story through a third party—which I never dreamed would get back to the church—provide the board with sufficient grounds to revoke my severance—a mere two months away from our baby's due date, and with no sign of future employment or income?

The full weight of the previous two weeks finally broke through the dam that had been restricting my emotions. My hat was the first to feel my rage, then my golf clubs— flying through the air across the parking lot—outpaced only by a flurry of expletives. Then came tears; so many tears. Later, Kyle and I would recall that moment as the first time in our friendship that I dropped "F-bombs" in his presence. He took the keys from me and drove us home as I called Kate, sobbing. I even remember leaving a voice mail at the church, pleading with them to not take away my severance.

The storm died down after a few days, and thankfully cooler heads prevailed. The church did not end up revoking my severance, but the whole ordeal felt like one more indication that the peace I so desperately sought by aligning my convictions with my actions would forever remain an illusion.

I'd sought integrity. I'd been honest about my spiritual journey. I'd come out as a full-on straight ally and stood up for my convictions. But for what? To be an outcast in my community and public enemy number one among my former staff and colleagues?

When Relationships Challenge Religion

The following week, Kate and I drove our boys west to San Diego hoping for a respite from the madness in the desert. At the conference, I met people I'd long respected, such as Doug Pagitt and Spencer Burke, as well as people who were just starting to make their voices heard, including Rachel Held Evans and Peter Rollins. It was a radical breath of fresh air to be surrounded by other progressive Christian types.

The first in-person conversation I had with Todd was in the nursery while Kate and I let our boys get some energy out after being in the car for seven hours. When the small talk concluded, he asked me, "So who was it?"

"Who was what?" I questioned.

"Was it a brother? A cousin? Who was the person close to you that came out of the closet and caused you to reevaluate your theology?"

"No one," I chuckled. "Assuming we become friends, you will officially be my first gay friend."

He was astounded as I explained that, for me, moving to a place of being an open and affirming Christian was the result of pursuing academic integrity and doing my best to follow where Christ was leading me.

As I've come to discover, the most common path people take toward the open and affirming position is when a relationship challenges their religion. Like how Carol, when I was ten, helped me see that gay people are not scary sinners who are a threat to Christianity. When someone's son, daughter, brother, sister, aunt, uncle, or whomever steps into their identity as LGBTQ, it can rupture previously held assumptions about faith and sexuality. This disruption forces people to ask hard questions about what they believe and why. And as they seek answers for how their loved one can be both gay and Christian, it isn't uncommon for new awareness and acceptance to take root in their hearts and minds.

I've heard recently that those in conservative Christian tribes are dismissing this type of journey toward being open and affirming. They argue that the person is making the move and changing theology only because they want to justify the life choices of the loved one. "No matter how noble that might be," they insist, "we can't let relationships trump the Word of God."

But what if the Bible itself presents this journey, where belief is challenged by experience and relationships, as an acceptable (or even, expected) mode of transformation?

For instance, when I read in Acts how the Gentile community was first integrated into the early church, I can't help but notice how relationships were forcing people to look inward about their prejudice and assumptions about what God was doing. The first Christians assumed this new movement, inaugurated by Jesus, would be a continuation of the Jewish story. But then Peter had an awakening about how God does not see the Gentiles as outsiders. This led Peter to enter the house of Cornelius, which broke Jewish purity laws because Cornelius was not a Jew. After spending a few moments with the Gentile man, Peter said, "I really am learning that God doesn't show partiality to one group of people over another" (Acts 10:34). Peter then preached the good news, causing the Holy Spirit to move through Cornelius and the other Gentiles in the house. Peter and his Jewish friends were astonished that the Spirit had been poured out—even on Gentiles—causing him to ask rhetorically, "These people have received the Holy Spirit just as we have. Surely no one can stop them from being baptized with water, can they?" (v. 47). Later, when Peter returned to Jerusalem, his fellow apostles criticized him for eating with Gentiles. But Peter told them the story of what happened and concluded with, "If God gave them the same gift he gave us who believed in the Lord Jesus Christ, then who am I? Could I stand in God's way?" (11:17).

An experience within the context of a relationship forced the early church to hold two truths together that seemed to be in conflict. Gentile people (seen as sinners and unclean) were professing allegiance to Jesus as Lord and, as a result, were showing the fruit of God's Spirit in their lives. This is the tension that many people have when loved ones in their lives identify as LGBTQ and are also card-carrying, Spirit-filled, fruit-producing followers of Jesus. The tension forces them to consider that maybe they have misused the Bible to condemn an entire people-group, denying them access to the grace of God.[4]

My journey toward becoming open and affirming was not like this, but I think it's important to honor those for whom it was. The Bible is full of stories of men and women whose beliefs were challenged and changed as a result of experiences that, on the surface, contradicted their theology. If we pay attention, I think relationships can be a monumental medium for the ongoing transformation through love in our lives.

A New Future Emerges

"What would it take," Todd said, as the waitress dropped off a basket of chips and salsa, "to get you to come out to San Diego and join our church?" It was the second day of the conference, and Todd had taken us out to lunch. Even though we'd just met, he was excited to talk about future ministry possibilities.

His words felt like that first night of sleeping in your own bed after weeks of travel, a fresh reminder that life won't always be about aching backs and exhaustion. There was someone out there, another Christian pastor, who saw me in my newly aligned self and wanted me. It felt too good to be true. "Todd, no offense, but you just met me. And I was fired four weeks ago." I don't know that I meant to respond like that, but I think it felt safer to dismiss his idea as nonsense, rather than expose myself to this unbelievable new possibility. Could I really have found a church home so quickly, where I could serve as a pastor and not need to keep my progressive theology a secret?

"I know," he went on, "but I think this could be a God thing. And I don't say that lightly." As Kate struggled to keep our three boys in their seats, I struggled to maintain a straight face. I couldn't believe this was happening. What he said next sealed the deal, and I knew this was where I wanted to be. "I'd love to bring you out to San Diego, have you join our staff as our Worship & Arts Pastor for a few years, and then transition you to become Lead Pastor." He explained that there were ideas brewing within the denomination about him moving on from the church to help plant other churches, and then he added, "Furthermore, I believe a family like yours could help take the church to the next level."

Little did Todd know that I had, for several years at that point, aspired to transition out of worship ministry and into full-time teaching and preaching. It felt like a dream job offer: a unicorn church (progressive with an evangelical vibe), located in San Diego, where I could do what I know and love, and—*at the same time*—work toward becoming a full-time preaching pastor. It felt like the nurse just came in and said, "Never mind, Mr. Martin, the dentist called and he isn't able to see you today. I guess you can go home. Oh, and your teeth have been magically cleaned." Maybe I wouldn't have to suffer the pain of unemployment. Maybe I wouldn't need to doubt my calling as a pastor. Maybe this was the plan the whole time.

The drive home, back to the tension-filled mess in Arizona, was a little less daunting after a few days in San Diego. We felt energized. I told Todd that I was excited to keep the conversation going. Kate was just as enthused as I was but hesitant to relocate our family. For her, if the church was in Oregon, where we'd be closer to family, it would be a no-brainer. But all that aside, even if San Diego wasn't in the cards for us, it was life-giving to know that I wasn't damaged goods.

We left California with a gift more valuable than a severance package, a community of friends, or a home in the suburbs.

We left with hope.

Moving, Healing, Beards, and More Moving

November rolled around, six weeks after I was fired, and Kate and I made the decision to move back to Oregon, lick our wounds, and try to figure out what to do next. We found a realtor who specialized in short sales, and we put our four-year-old home on the market; we'd eventually sell for tens of thousands less than we built it for. We emailed friends and family back home to let them know our plan. And we stared at a calendar, circling the date five months in the future, when our severance package—our sole source of income—would come to an end.

We packed up our house (except for our brand-new washer and dryer and a bunch of kids toys, because, well, the moving company didn't bring a large enough truck), loaded up the minivan with our three boys, my mom, our dog, a fish bowl, Kate, myself, and suitcases with enough supplies for a couple weeks, and began the trek north.

November and December of that year proved to be two of the most important months for me. I made the decision to lean all the way into my pain and doubts. For two months, I didn't shave, calling it my "Depression Beard."[5] During that time, I grieved and mourned the loss of friends, the loss of work, and the loss of hope in the Christian church. I stopped going to church, didn't bother praying, and spent my days at home playing with my boys. Looking back, I believe my healing process would have taken much longer had I not been intentional about going through the trauma of what happened. Not ignoring it, or pressing on, or taking up some Christian cliché about "all things working together for good," or "let go and let God." I didn't want to smile and pretend that everything was okay. Or that I was okay. I wasn't. And I think my willingness to be honest with that, to be okay with not being okay, is what allowed me to move through it and then beyond it. As the pattern goes, resurrection comes only *after* death. And I did not want to ignore or attempt to expedite my time in the tomb.

When the new year rolled around, shortly after our fourth son was born, I was ready to rejoin the land of the living. I shaved my beard and began looking for work. Not church work, mind you, just a job to pay the bills. Being back in Salem meant that I had plenty of contacts; which led to a lot of promising meetings and interviews. But I'd never had to look for work before, especially in the non-church world. And it was a harsh reality when I realized that non-ministry organizations have no metric for evaluating the worth of a pastor. My résumé, with naught but seven years of being a working pastor, did not communicate how valuable an asset I could be. So week after week came and went, and all I had to show for it were a dozen meetings over sandwiches and coffee.

With only little more than a month left in my severance package, Kate and I started to panic. We sat in the parking lot of Target one afternoon when I mentioned to Kate, "Oh yeah, I need to call James back."

"Who is James?"

"He's the executive director at that church in San Diego. He's been calling me, trying to get closure on whether or not we're interested in moving down there. I need to call him back and let him know they can officially move on and take me off their list."

"Wait," Kate said, as she stared out the front window.

I did a double take. It was no secret that I still wanted to explore San Diego, but Kate had not felt the same. She felt that uprooting our family again would be too much. Plus, I think she knew that going immediately to another church context would not have been wise. And she wasn't wrong. It's clear to me now that we needed each of the six months we spent in Oregon. Those were healing months, grounding months. They gave us time to get more clear about who we were and what we wanted.

So communications with Todd had stopped. I had explained that, while their offer sounded wonderful, we couldn't accept it. But I guess they had a hard time taking no for an answer, and I got a call from James out of the blue in March, making one last plea. Had I called him back right away and reiterated our decision to stay in Oregon, there's no telling where our lives would be at this point. But I forgot. And a few days went by. Now here Kate and I were, in Target's parking lot, discussing San Diego for the first time in months.

"What do you mean, wait?" I asked, nonplussed by the possible turn of events.

"Let's not make that call just yet. I think we might need to re-explore the possibility of San Diego," she explained. "You haven't been able to find work, and besides, more than that, I know you, Colby. I know that, even though you'd be willing to not work in ministry so that our family can eat, you were born to pastor people. That's who you are. That's what you do."

It took almost two years after that conversation in Target before Kate shared the entirety of what was going on for her that day, what it meant for her to open the door to San Diego. Virtually every component of Kate's life dreams involved living in Oregon, so giving that up and moving out of state (again) for the sake of what I wanted, was/is a gift of love deeper than I deserve.

And so the next few days we talked: Kate and I; James and I; Todd, Kate, and I. We asked our boys how they might feel ("Well," our oldest said, "it's hard to decide . . . on the one hand, in Oregon, we have family . . . but on the other, there's Sea World!"). We decided to fly down and spend a weekend interviewing for the position, unprepared for the beauty of the diverse community. One of their taglines is, "The church you never thought existed, but always hoped had," and we couldn't agree more. We felt loved the minute we arrived, as the staff and elders were delighted by our family and thrilled at what it could mean for their church if we joined them. I was anxious about their ability to afford me—supporting a family of six in Southern California is not easy. But a week after we flew home from the interview they told us that they raised enough money to guarantee a salary for the first two years, with the hopes that I could help grow the church to pay for my position. It seemed like a perfect match, and all the ducks were lining up. In the final hour, it seemed we had found our next move and found our next church home.

So on April 30, the last day we had coverage from my severance package, with our bank account literally down to double digits, we loaded the van back up (this time with four kids) and made the trek back south.

After years of living out of alignment, unable to express myself and be honest about my beliefs, I couldn't wait to see what ministry was like in a context where I didn't have to hide. I was anxious to once again lead worship, curate an arts ministry, and preach to a community made up of the entire range of spiritual seekers: gay, straight, man, woman, Anglo, African, Latino, Christian, agnostic, conservative, progressive, and so on.

For the first year or so, I was convinced we had at last found the unicorn church. But soon it became clear to Kate and me that, in spite of holding great promise, this new church in San Diego was not a good place for us. It was an unstable environment that did not respond well to questions about its own lack of health. Yes, my theological self felt more at home and more aligned. But the pastoral part of me, the part that chases after the abundant, flourishing life found in the Spirit, was stifled. And my passion to call other people into wholehearted living was met with mistrust and disdain. Between the leadership and myself were competing ideas as to what it meant and what it looked like to be a pastor and to shepherd people.

So while it was a great place to reenter ministry after the trauma of my firing, and it showed me that churches and people do exist who are progressive and Christian,

Kate and I were ultimately drawn by something stronger, something more compelling and beautiful.

Which is why, twenty months after we arrived in San Diego, we started something brand new, from the ground up.

The unicorn church, I was discovering, is more expansive than simply being open and affirming and worshiping Jesus with guitars and drums. That is just the tip of the horn . . . er . . . iceberg.

What I truly longed for was deeper than that: a faith community where people could come alive in the same sort of way that I was. Where who we are and what we believe on the inside matches the life we live and the people we love and want to do life with on the outside. Where a community chases after the vision of Kingdom-living together, with a spirit of authenticity, vulnerability, and trust. Where grace permeates every interaction and animates every person as we invite one another in to wholehearted living.

It was time to take all the lessons learned from the churches I had served, where integrated living hadn't been an option and where painful exits still left wounds, and start to clear away the rubble, lay down new foundations, and allow a more beautiful dream to rise from the ashes.

CHAPTER 8

→

RECONCILING A FRACTURED COMMUNITY

Romans 1:26–27

The other day I had coffee with Josh. Josh is from Texas but was visiting San Diego and wanted to meet with me. He said that he found some of my writings and videos online, was grateful for my ministry, and would love to tell me his story, believing I would be a safe and understanding audience.[1] We met up for coffee, found some privacy in the back patio, and made quick work of the requisite small talk before getting right to it.

Josh had known he was gay since he was young. However, being raised a pastor's kid in a conservative Christian household meant he had to keep his thoughts and feelings to himself. Growing up, he never fit in like his brothers did, and he never connected with his father like he longed to. In high school, he found a passion for theater and began dreaming about life as an artist—singing and dancing on stage. The other kids noticed he was different, and it became their goal to ensure that Josh always knew he didn't belong. The constant bullying forced him to transition to homeschooling. My heart ached as he talked about "giving up his dreams," resigning to the fact that a career in the theater would never be his life.

As an adult, he listened to the counsel of his conservative religious leaders who told him he was damaged, and he spent years in ex-gay therapy as a result.[2] When that didn't "work," he found a woman to marry because, as he told me that morning, he believed it might be "the missing piece to take away the gay."

Of course, his feelings and attractions never did change. Now, a dozen years later, he and his wife had an incredible eight-year-old daughter and, as he told me that morning, had begun the process of trying to figure out how to reconcile his reality as a gay man with the fact that they were married and had a family.

The last part of Josh's story I want to mention is this: He told me that he had, over the previous year, consumed a lot of biblical scholarship on the Clobber Passages. The most helpful for him turned out to be my series of UnClobber videos because, as he put it, "You are not gay. You don't have a dog in the fight. For some reason your words, your arguments, landed differently for me." I thanked him for his kind words, but then he added this, "However, I still can't get past Romans. The Old Testament passages are no problem, and the two verses in Corinthians and Timothy seem easy to explain. But I can't yet get past the passage in Romans that appears to condemn me as a gay man."

You are not alone, Josh.

The two verses in question, in Paul's letter to the church in Rome, are where many good-hearted Christians come up short in their efforts toward full inclusion and affirmation of the LGBTQ community. The passage in question has been misused to label countless young boys and girls as unnatural, abnormal, and broken. They have been the shrapnel to pop the hopes and dreams of the Joshes of the world. I told Josh that Romans was also the final domino to fall for me. It was the most challenging to look at with fresh eyes; to consider that it might not mean what I've always thought it meant.

Romans was the place where I spent the most time wondering, "Is there any other way through this? Do these two verses have the singular power to hold back millions of men, women, and children from full inclusion in the Kingdom of God? Do these two verses contain the key to the lock that keeps our gay siblings from being members and leaders in our churches? If all else can be UnClobbered, are we ultimately left defeated at the doorstep of Rome; content to lay down our Pride flags, turn around, and stumble home; admitting that yes, in fact, the church has historically been correct in its posture toward those born with same-sex attraction?"

Though it took me a while to get here, I now answer those questions with a passionate and reasoned "No!"

A Fresh Reading of Romans

Because this will be the most dense chapter, let me offer a brief outline of where we are going.

First, I will unpack the historical context of Romans to give us the necessary grounding for understanding what Paul was hoping to accomplish with his letter. Then, in the largest section of this chapter, I will spend time exploring the broader passage (Rom. 1:18–32) that holds the two Clobber verses. The importance of grasping what Paul was doing here cannot be overstated. Third, I will extract some of the specific words and phrases used in the Clobber Passage and show what, in their context, was being described. Finally, I will pull it all together, and we'll discover not only that we have misunderstood and misused this Clobber Passage but also that what waits for us on the other side is a profound challenge to expand our hearts and minds and allow the gospel, which is "the power of God for salvation," to have its transformative way in us.

I still remember the first time I semi-sort of participated in something that could barely be described as yoga. It was dreadful. In a room full of other people, I was asked to move my body and limbs in ways I'd never considered moving them. Awkward and bumping into people next to me, I was hyperaware of the unnatural positions my body was failing to contort to. Plus, having a *New York Times* best-selling author celebrity sitting next to me made me even more self-conscious. And yet, even though my embarrass-o-meter was peaking, I stuck with it until the end.

What I discovered was a surprising freedom on the other end. After all was said and done, I was glad I stuck with it, even though I wanted to bail because of how ridiculous I felt and how uncomfortable it was.

I say that because I'm anticipating that some of you might need to imagine me awkwardly doing yoga . . . wait, scratch that . . . I mean, I invite you to read this chapter and expect that some parts of it might feel like a stretch to you. Some parts might feel uncomfortable or absurd, and you may be tempted to check out. But my hope is that you hang in there until the end and see if maybe there might just be a way to understand Paul in this all-too-familiar passage that doesn't result in a blanket condemnation of homosexuality.

So, first things first: What was going on in Rome, and why did Paul write them a letter?

A Church Divided

From historical sources other than the Bible, we know the sociopolitical climate of Rome just prior to when Paul wrote his letter. In the year AD 49, the Roman Emperor Claudius expelled the Jews from Rome because the Jews were "constantly rioting at the instigation of Chrestus,"[3] meaning Jesus Christ. So between AD 49 and 54 (when Claudius eventually died), the Jewish people—including Jewish Christians—were expelled from the city. This made a significant impact on the house churches in Rome. Prior to AD 49, the churches would have been a mixture of Jewish and Gentile Christians, but for a five-year period, the churches consisted of only Gentiles. Without their Jewish members, the churches were bound to experience change. So when the edict ended upon Claudius' death and the Jewish Christians returned home, there would have been inevitable conflict with regard to how the churches were run, who was in charge, and so on.

It is to this conflicted community, fractured along ethnic lines, that Paul wrote his letter. One of his primary goals was to offer a theological exposition of the gospel that reminded the church in Rome to see one another as equals at God's Table. With a solid foundation—and reminder—of what the gospel was all about, Paul could then move toward fostering reconciliation between the Jewish and Gentile Christians.

Contrary to what is sometimes believed (indeed, what I believed for most of my religious life), Romans is not an abstract thesis of Paul's theology. It was not written so that Christianity for all time would have a theological explanation of the doctrine of justification by faith (even if the letter contains some of that). Nor is it a universal letter designed to offer timeless truths about the gospel (even if the letter contains some of that, too). Rather, it is a letter grounded in history, written by Paul to a particular faith community in Rome for a specific purpose.[4]

In part, Paul wrote Romans to explain the gospel in a way that made sense of his mission to be the apostle to the Gentiles. The Gentiles, as Paul writes in one of the climactic moments in the letter, were the wild olive shoots grafted into the branch, aka Israel, demonstrating God's mercy to all humanity (see Rom. 11:17, 32). This created a theological justification for Paul's missionary efforts, because the Kingdom of God was open to all, both Jews and Gentiles (see Rom. 1:16). And yet here was a community that was threatening to undo that project because they were divided along ethnic lines. In his letter, Paul was pushing, pulling, and at times kicking the fractured community toward reconciliation, with repeated admonishments to not judge one another but to live in harmony (see Rom. 12:5). Only when we hold this backdrop for Romans in our minds as we read the text will we ensure that we give ourselves the best opportunity to understand what Paul was saying and why.

A Question for Consideration

Before we examine the section of Romans in which the Clobber Passage is found and ask how it is that Romans 1:18–32 contributes to Paul's goal of bringing together the fractured Roman church, let me pause and say this: There is compelling reason to believe that these fifteen verses were not written by, or at least original to, Paul. The composition, word choice, and overall flow of the Greek are notably un-Pauline in comparison to the rest of his body of work.

Now, you might be tempted to check out at this point, like I wanted to with yoga. But hang in there. It wasn't uncommon for Paul to drop in well-known quotes and ideas not original to himself into his letters, trusting that his audience would recognize them as such (e.g., see 1 Cor. 10:23; 15:33; Titus 1:12; and from his missionary work, Acts 17:28). It is possible, then, that Paul inserts this self-contained argument—that outlines the plight of the pagans, as we'll see—from an outside source.

But whether Paul borrowed these fifteen verses from another source, was inspired by an outside source, or wrote it himself using a style and voicing unlike his own, here is the question I want to consider: Did Paul agree with the content of these verses?

I admit this is a bizarre question. But I think it's important, as will become clear. The traditional perspective on this Clobber Passage assumes that *of course* these are Paul's words, and so *of course* they reflect his beliefs. It is believed that they articulate Paul's position toward same-sex sex acts, namely that they are the result of wickedness and depravity.

But what if something else is going on? What if Paul has a larger (and different) purpose in mind?

You Have Heard It Said

I want to show how this Clobber Passage was part of a larger rhetorical device Paul used to lay a foundation for his argument that the Jewish Christians were no better (or worse) than the Gentile Christians in Rome. To set up his argument, Paul offers a brief introduction to his understanding of the gospel:

> For I am not ashamed of the gospel, for it is the power of God for salvation to everyone who believes, to the Jew first and also to the Greek. For in it the righteousness of God is revealed from faith for faith, as it is written, "The righteous shall live by faith." (Rom. 1:16–17 ESV)

Already you hear Paul advocating that the good news of Jesus means salvation for everyone, both Jew and Greek. All Christians in Rome who hear this letter from Paul should breathe in deep the truth that Jesus' inauguration of God's Kingdom on earth as it is in heaven is an invitation for all people. The tone has been set.

Then, our section in question begins,

> For the wrath of God is revealed from heaven against all ungodliness and unrighteousness of men, who by their unrighteousness suppress the truth. For what

can be known about God is plain to them, because God has shown it to them. (vv. 18–19 ESV)

What comes next, over the following thirteen verses, is an extrapolation of how these people—the "wicked and ungodly"—knew about God but did not honor God. We hear how they exchanged the glory of God for images of mortal beings and how, in turn, God gave them over to their sinful desires like sexual impurity and degrading their bodies. We are told that they exchanged the truth of God for a lie and worship the created rather than the Creator.

And then, as a result of their turning away from God, God gave them over to shameful things. This is where we arrive at the Clobber Passage:

> For this reason God gave them up to dishonorable passions. For their women exchanged natural relations for those that are contrary to nature; and the men likewise gave up natural relations with women and were consumed with passion for one another, men committing shameless acts with men and receiving in themselves the due penalty for their error. (vv. 26–27 ESV)

The section continues, describing how these ungodly people gave up their knowledge of God altogether, which leads to a depraved mind, and as a result, they were filled with every kind of wickedness, evil, and depravity. It concludes with a list of not-so-kind descriptions of who these wicked people would become. In short, zero punches are pulled in describing a group of people who have received the wrath of God poured out upon them.

When taken at face value and understood in the traditional perspective, it come as no surprise that countless Christian leaders—with large platforms and wide influence—have blamed tragedies in our world like earthquakes, tsunamis, and mass shootings on the depravity of those engaged in same-sex sexual behavior. This section from Romans 1 does not paint a great picture of what it looks like when God's wrath is poured out on wicked people. And when it *seems* that sitting right in the middle of this section are words condemning people who engage in same-sex sex acts, it can feel a bit unsettling.

But *ought* we take this section at face value? To return to our earlier question, should these fifteen verses be understood as Paul's own thoughts, feelings, and beliefs about wicked people who turn their backs on God? Should we therefore read this and take from it a definitive Pauline opinion on how God feels about people who engage in same-sex sex acts?

I don't think so. And here's why.

These fifteen verses are what is called a "self-contained discourse," a sort of prefabricated argument if you will. Paul leverages this discourse as a rhetorical device to make a larger point. And that point, as I'm about to show, is not linked to Paul's own thinking about wicked and ungodly people.

Do you recall how Jesus, in the Gospels, would sometimes say, "you have heard it said, but I say to you . . ."? Hold that concept in your mind as we move forward, because I believe Paul was making a similar move.

A quick word from Aristotle and Solomon should help explain.

Heaping Blame and Hoisting Boundaries

In *Art of Rhetoric,* Aristotle's treatise on the art of persuasion, he detailed what he called the three branches of rhetorical discourse. One such branch he called epideictic discourse. Speakers used this particular mode of persuasion to either praise or blame an individual or group. Of particular note for us, if the goal of the discourse was to heap blame, then the speaker would rally the audience around a shared hatred for a common enemy. Think of speeches given by presidential candidates every four years. Aristotle believed that the "epideictic style is especially suited to written compositions, for its function is reading."[5]

Paul was well-versed in rhetoric, and scholars have long seen its influence in his letters, including our section here in Romans 1:18–32. As it turns out, this self-contained discourse matches the tone, structure, and purpose of an epideictic discourse. In other words, these fifteen verses were composed to persuade the readers (or, since these letters were often read aloud to churches, the *listeners*) to heap blame on the wicked and ungodly people that this passage was describing.

Why does that matter? Because instead of isolating two verses (26 and 27) that appear to condemn homosexuality, we need to step back and grasp the context in a way that illuminates what was being communicated. Understanding that these two verses are part of a larger section, composed with the goal of whipping up an emotional response in the original hearers—an epideictic discourse—will change how we understand them.

Furthermore, not only is this self-contained discourse modeled as an epideictic discourse, it is also subversively similar (if not altogether derivative) of passages found in the Wisdom of Solomon.

The Wisdom of Solomon was a well-known and widely circulated book written from within Judaism, sometime between the second century BC to AD 40. The goal of the book, often called simply Wisdom, was, in part, to strengthen the divide between Jews and Gentiles; to remind the Jewish people that God was *for* them and *against* the pagan nations. One of the key points in Wisdom was to lay out the plot line for depravity among the Gentiles. It went like this:

Gentiles failed to know God → turned to idolatry → engaged in immorality → and received due punishment.

This natural theology was the standard operating procedure for the Jewish community during the time of the New Testament.

Perhaps you noticed the similarities of that plot line with those found in our fifteen-verse self-contained discourse? The tone, language, and arguments of Romans 1:18–32 are nearly identical to those found in Wisdom. And this was intentional. The goal was not only to whip up a strong emotional response of blame (epideictic discourse) but also to bring to mind the familiar beliefs and assumptions held within Judaism about the inferiority of the Gentile world.

Paul uses (borrows? writes?) this discourse that echoes the Wisdom of Solomon to evoke the prejudices of the Jewish Christians in Rome. You and I, reading our Bibles at home, would likely not pick up on this (unless you regularly read from the Wisdom of Solomon, I suppose). But Paul would have correctly assumed that the audience in Rome would recognize the themes, tone, and rhetoric.

Springing the Trap

Now that we know *what* this passage in Romans 1 is, let's look at *why* Paul inserted this discourse as he did. In other words, why was Paul stirring up deeply entrenched prejudices held by Jewish people for Gentiles, especially if his ultimate goal was to reconcile the community that was fractured along ethnic lines?

The key to understanding why Paul used the discourse is found in the very next verse after our passage, which kicks off chapter 2:

Therefore you have no excuse, O man, every one of you who judges. For in passing judgment on another you condemn yourself, because you, the judge, practice the very same things. (Rom. 2:1 ESV)

After fifteen verses aimed at idolatrous pagans, loaded with multiple uses of the evocative third person "they," Paul now flips the script and goes second person, "therefore *you* have no excuse . . . every one of *you* who judges . . . *you* condemn yourself . . . *you*, the judge, practice the same things" (emphasis added).

What's going on here? What is Paul doing, and why? And what (you might be wondering) does this have to do with homosexuality?

We're almost there. I promise.

In order for Paul to get where he wants to go (uniting the Jewish and Gentile Christians), he must first level the playing field. He must establish that neither group is superior to the other. He must unearth long-held prejudices, expose them, and bring everyone to mindfulness of their sameness. To do this, he sets a trap for the Jewish Christians. He launches into a discourse that taps into their prejudices toward their Gentile neighbors, stringing them along as though he sympathizes with their posture.

You can imagine the energy in the room crescendoing as the reader of the letter tells the story of wicked people (i.e., Gentiles) who turn from God, move toward idolatry, engage in immoral acts, and reap God's judgment. You can picture the Jewish Christians in the room turning to one another, slapping each other on the back, congratulating themselves that Paul is on *their* side, the *right* side. As Paul's opening words give the Jewish Christians the ammo to re-establish their power and positions in the churches, you can feel the Gentile Christians panic, wondering if maybe they had been confused about the "good" part of the good news.

But then Paul, after luring his audience inside his snare, flicks the trigger and reveals his purpose. He pivots from speaking *about* Gentiles to speaking *at* the Jews, insisting that they are no different, and certainly no better. In passing judgment on the Gentiles within their community, they have revealed that they are in the same boat. If the Gentiles (according to popular Jewish prejudice, not according to

Paul) suppressed the truth of God by their unrighteousness (1:18), then the Jews (according now to Paul) must acknowledge that they suppress the truth of God by judging the Gentiles (2:1). The playing field has been leveled, as Paul summarizes in chapter 3,

> What then? Are we Jews any better off? No, not at all. For we have already charged that all, both Jews and Greeks, are under sin, as it is written: "None is righteous, no, not one; no one understands; no one seeks for God. (Rom. 3:9–10 ESV)

The immediate shift in chapter 2 is where Paul turns his attention to the Jewish Christians who would have found nothing objectionable in the discourse of 1:18–32. Biblical scholar Calvin Porter puts it like this: "The shift to the direct address, the second person singular, along with the coordinating conjunction 'therefore,' indicates that the reader who agrees with or is responsible for the discourse in 1:18-32 is now the person being addressed by Paul."[6]

Allow me to say that again: if you were a Jewish Christian in Rome and you agreed in any way with the Jewish prejudices and erroneous beliefs about the plight of the Gentiles (as articulated in places like the Wisdom of Solomon, and now reiterated here in Romans 1:18–32), then Paul is calling *you* out as being the source of the problem.

It's as though Paul says, "There is no excusing you when you throw around judgments like that discourse I just recited, because when you judge the Gentiles you are condemning yourself!" Throughout the rest of the letter Paul emphasizes that the fractured communities need to stop judging one another, because judgment is God's and God's alone (see Rom. 14:12–13).

In his opening chapters, Paul addresses how the traditional Jewish perspective of the Gentile world is, in and of itself, an enemy to the gospel. This perspective, found in 1:18–32, stands in opposition to Paul's Gentile mission, and adds fuel to the fire in the already-fractured community. So starting with chapter 2, he begins to explain how the ideas in 1:18–32 are not in keeping with the gospel he is preaching. In other words, he spends time in chapters 2–4 undoing the arguments and assumptions as stated in 1:18–32.

For instance:

— The discourse suggests that God's wrath is revealed now against ungodliness (1:18); but Paul refutes that by saying that God's wrath and judgment are yet to come (2:5–6).
— The discourse declares that God has specific judgment toward the Gentile people; but Paul refutes that by later saying that God shows no partiality (2:9–11).
— The discourse tells of a God who gives up on people, and gives them over to wickedness and to death (1:24, 26, 28); but Paul refutes that by declaring that "God gives life to the dead and calls into existence the things that do not exist" (4:17).

As Porter puts it, "Romans 1:18-32 consists of a discourse used in the life of a community to establish, maintain and strengthen the community's boundaries when those are threatened. Romans 2:1-16, on the other hand, consists of part of Paul's refutation of that discourse and its attendant practices."[7]

In summary, the self-contained discourse that Paul utilized in Romans 1:18–32 was representative of the typical posture of Jews toward Gentiles. Paul argued that this sort of posture worked against the gospel, and he insisted that if the Jewish Christians in Rome resonated with the posture of the discourse, then *they* were the problem. They were just as guilty of suppressing God's truth, via their judgmental beliefs, as they maintained the Gentiles were in their supposed unrighteous living.[8]

So when we step back and consider that the Clobber Passage resides inside this discourse, we can no longer say with certainty that the words do, in fact, reflect Paul's personal beliefs about same-sex sex acts. Instead, what we *can* say is that they reflect the larger attitude and belief of first-century Jews about pagan Gentiles. It's a nasty, judgmental attitude, at that, which Paul adamantly proclaims does not reflect the truth of God or the fullness of the good news.

Dishonorable, Unnatural, and Shameless

The question still remains: Does this self-contained discourse, fashioned after the Jewish prejudices of the Wisdom of Solomon, reflect Paul's personal convictions about the plight of the pagan? Can we deduce with certainty that Paul believed that Gentiles were ungodly, unrighteous people who turned their backs on God and were, as a result, given over to a depraved state?

More to the point, would Paul have agreed with the sentiment behind the Clobber Passages?

On one hand, that is beside the point. In asking this question, we are missing the forest for the trees. It seems to me that, rather than Paul describing his opinion on ungodly living, he is doing as I've suggested: exposing the Jewish prejudice and leveling the playing field in an attempt to foster reconciliation. On the other hand, we can keep going deeper into verses 26 and 27 and discover that they neither provide a blanket condemnation of homosexuality nor give biblical grounds to condemn any and all same-sex sex acts. I want to explore three parts of these verses, and they're emphasized below:

For this reason God gave them up to *dishonorable passions*. For their women exchanged natural relations for those that are *contrary to nature*; and the men likewise gave up natural relations with women and were consumed with passion for one another, men committing *shameless acts* with men and receiving in themselves the due penalty for their error. (Rom. 1:26–27 ESV)

Dishonorable Passions

First, from verse 26, "God gave them over to dishonorable passions." The word here translated as "dishonorable" in the ESV and "degrading" in the CEB and NRSV is the Greek word *atimia*, which other translations take in a much more morally charged direction such as "evil" or "vile." But if something was *atimia*, it was not so much about being morally reprehensible, it was about being culturally shameful. It was about bringing dishonor to a person or family. Additionally, if used in the court of law, if something was deemed *atimia*, it was because it had no value or worth.

To commit *atimia*, then, was to engage in a behavior that had no value and would bring shame and dishonor upon you. It was a violation of a cultural custom. This should bring to mind our discussion from chapter 6 about actions that were *toevah*. Similar to *toevah*, it would be a mistake to assume that *atimia* was something inherently wrong or sinful. For instance, Paul also said to the church in Corinth, "Does not even nature teach you that if a man wears long hair it is a disgrace [*atimia*] for him?" (1 Cor. 11:14 ESV). Having long hair was not, and is not, morally reprehensible. It is not vile or evil. But in that culture it was seen as dishonorable, an act that violated the cultural custom of the day.[9]

So, in this self-contained discourse of popular Jewish prejudice, Paul (or the original author) demonstrated how Gentiles were engaged in acts that clearly went against Jewish cultural customs. They were *atimia* — dishonorable, shameful — like how, in America, it is dishonorable and shameful to allow the American flag to touch the ground.

No one would suggest that such an action is inherently evil, or that it offends the nature of God. But in our culture, it is a shameful act.

Shameless Acts

Next, from verse 27, "the men . . . were consumed with passion for one another, men committing shameless acts with men." The word here translated as "shameless" in many translations is the Greek word *aschemosune*, and it describes behavior that was unseemly or indecent. The situation being described is men, being overtaken by their passions, engaging in same-sex sex acts that were possibly performed in public spaces or in conjunction with pagan temple idol worship. Both of those would have certainly been considered unseemly and indecent.

As I will explain further in chapter 10, I am not suggesting that Paul never wrote harsh words of judgment against sexual behavior by two people of the same sex (or opposite sex, for that matter). What I am arguing for is a more nuanced position that sees Paul as condemning the forms of same-sex sex acts (again, see chapter 10) that would have been most prevalent in his day; but that we ought not take those particular prohibitions from two thousand years ago and use them as a blanket condemnation for any and all sex acts today.

The "shameless" acts mentioned here in Romans 1:27, like the exploitive acts I'll cover in chapter 10 from 1 Corinthians 6:9, are outside the bounds of good and healthy expressions of sexual activity. When taken together with the dishonorable acts from verse 26, what emerges is a (heavily prejudiced Jewish) picture of Gentiles who have rejected God, turned toward idolatry, and been given over to distorted sexual practices that offend and are contrary to Jewish purity laws and cleanliness customs. Any average first-century Jew would find these sex acts shameful and indecent. Matthew Vines, in his book *God and the Gay Christian*, makes a compelling argument that these shameless acts were done as a result of men being "consumed with passion." In other words, they were not acting out of a place of love and mutuality, but out of desire for excess.[10]

Today, we know that homosexuality is a sexual orientation from birth. We also can conceive of two people of the same sex who love each other and choose to be in a relationship where they see each other as equals, where there is a mutually honoring and respecting dynamic between them. These concepts—a person's sexual orientation, and egalitarian same-sex relationships—simply did not exist in the ancient world. So you would be hard-pressed to argue that this self-contained discourse in Romans 1:18–32 speaks against homosexuality as an orientation, same-sex sex acts engaged within the context of mutuality and love, or marriage between two people of the same sex.

If we are searching for biblical words to inform us of how God might feel about gays and lesbians, this passage is helpful only insofar as it conveys to us the feelings and beliefs of the Jewish community toward the Gentile community who engaged in idolatrous, exploitive, and culturally offensive sex acts.

Contrary to Nature

The third phrase I want to unpack is the idea of women exchanging natural relations for those that are "contrary to nature" or "unnatural." The Greek phrase in question is *para phusis*, meaning "against nature." The traditional interpretation argues that as a result of abandoning God and turning toward idolatry, the Gentiles in question were exchanging natural sexual relations for those that went against nature. In this perspective, God's design (according to the creation account in Genesis, affirmed later in Leviticus, and again here by Paul) is for men to have sex with women. That is the natural way. Any other sexual expression is unnatural and against God's design and intention. Therefore, as a result of its unnaturalness, it is inherently sinful.

However, in its simplest explanation, the best way to understand *para phusis* (and its converse, *kata phusis*, "according to nature"), with regard to what the concept meant at the time and in the context of sexual relations, has to do with whether or not sexual activity was procreative. In other words, a male and female having sexual intercourse was "according to nature" because it had the potential for procreation, rendering all other sexual expressions "against nature."

The root of the phrases *kata/para phusis* goes back to Plato, is picked up three hundred years later by Philo (a Jewish philosopher), and then lands in the lap of this discourse in Romans. The thread of what constitutes *kata/para phusis* is consistent: sexual intercourse between a man and woman is "according to nature" if, and only if, it is procreative. It wasn't about the morality of the act. This is not to say that some sexual activity wouldn't still be seen as morally offensive—clearly that's not the case. Rather, my point is to draw attention to what constituted whether something was "according to" or "contrary to" nature.

Illustrating this point, Augustine wrote that a man having sex with a prostitute, while not praiseworthy in the slightest, was nonetheless "according to nature." It was not moral, but at least it was natural. Then he said, "But if one has relations even with one's wife in a part of the body which was not made for begetting children, such relations are against nature and indecent."[11]

This matters because Romans 1:26 has traditionally been seen as the Bible's solitary place of condemnation against lesbianism. But this is neither what the text says nor how the early church understood Paul's words.

Women exchanging natural relations (i.e., procreative sexual acts) for those that are contrary to nature (i.e., non-procreative sexual acts) most certainly was intended to mean anal heterosexual sex with men, not sexual relations between two women. Up through the fourth century, church fathers who commented on Romans 1:26 understood Paul in this way. Not referring to lesbianism, but referring to men and women having sex in unnatural ways (that is, non-procreative sexual intercourse).

Then, as verse 27 begins with "likewise," the argument continues on to men who forsook the "natural use of the woman" (KJV) and committed *aschemosune*, the shameless acts mentioned above.

So, what we can say is that men having sex with men (also men having anal/oral sex with women) was seen as contrary to nature in the ancient Jewish perspective because it was non-procreative. *After* that, we could have the discussion about the morality or the sinfulness of such sexual activity; but the two must be separated.

We are laying down a land mine to trip over later if we insist that *para phusis* is a description of behavior that is inherently immoral. In Romans 11, Paul closes in on his theological argument for the full inclusion of Gentiles in the family of God, and he uses the imagery of grafting a branch onto an olive tree. In his metaphor, the olive tree is Israel and the branches that God grafts in are the Gentiles. Paul says that God grafted them in—you guessed it—*para phusis*. For God to include the Gentiles into the family was a move against nature. Therefore, it stands to reason that just because a particular action in the Bible is called "contrary to nature" cannot inherently imply that it is evil and wicked, otherwise, according to Paul, God acted in evil and wicked ways.

Romans 1:26–27 is not an indictment of people who are born with same-sex attraction, as though loving someone of the same sex violates the morality of natural law. Instead, what we find is an explanation of how the Jewish people saw the plight of godless pagans, who turned their backs on the One True Creator God and instead embraced idolatry. The most common example of the wickedness of idolatrous pagans was their sexual immorality, acts that were shameful and offensive to Jewish sensibilities, and were called into question because they went against nature by being non-procreative.

The Acts in Question

One final thought about this Clobber Passage.

In the Greco-Roman world were numerous temples dedicated to countless gods and goddesses. Archaeology has helped us assemble a decent picture of what life looked like in and around these temples, and sexual rituals and activity were central components. In any given temple, you could find both male and female prostitutes engaged in cultic rituals involving orgies and idol worship. The non-procreative sex acts (men with other men, or anal/oral sex) practiced by idol-worshiping pagans were viewed as culturally offensive to the Jewish people and were engaged in shameless and indecent ways. They were a result of men and women refusing to honor God, and they were a result of people gorging on excess and yielding to their selfish passions and lust.

That is the environment and activity that books like the Wisdom of Solomon and discourses like Romans 1:18–32 aimed at in their condemnation of the pagan world.

What I want to ask you now, dear reader, is if the above description matches any friends or family members you might have who identify as gay *and* Christian?

To say that differently, imagine young men and women who, like Josh from above, have known all their lives that they are gay. As they grow, they become consumed by the love and grace of God through Jesus, and they devote their lives to bringing glory and honor to him. They serve in the church, they love the least of these, they give to the poor and needy. They practice ancient disciplines like prayer, Bible reading, fasting, and meditation. They are patient, kind, generous, and compassionate.

But (unlike dear Josh) they are in loving, committed same-sex relationships.

I ask you, what do a few verses about people accused of turning their backs on God, worshiping idols, and giving in to their lusts, have to say to them?

I believe the answer is "nothing."

The Romans Clobber Passage—though on the surface, admittedly the toughest of all—simply does not stand up to scrutiny. It does not supply the church with grounds for shaming boys and girls who are attracted to the same sex. It does not arm the church with ammo for launching campaigns of hate and discrimination against the LGBTQ community. And it does not hold the key to keep the doors of our churches locked, excluding our gay and lesbian siblings from full membership and participation in the Kingdom of God.

For It Is the Power of God for Salvation

I long for a day when young boys and girls don't have to hide who they are or give up on their dreams because they are gay. I long for a day when men and women don't marry the wrong gendered person, because they think they have to or because they think it will fix them, and then years later have to navigate how to (or if to) slowly dismantle a family. I long for a day when gay Christians are not seen as godless pagans who have turned their backs on their faith, their Lord, and their church.

Paul wrote a letter to a church in Rome almost two thousand years ago. The church was struggling because the Jewish Christians and the Gentile Christians couldn't find harmony. They were constantly judging one another. So Paul, leveraging his skill in the art of rhetoric, exposed the prejudices of the Jewish Christians and argued that their inflammatory and judgmental posture toward Gentiles was working against his very mission and indeed was working against the foundation of the gospel. Confusion has since come because the church decided to interpret two verses in this letter as being Paul's condemnation of any and all same-sex sex acts, instead of seeing them as part of a larger discourse typical of how Jews saw their Gentile neighbors. And, in a tragic twist, these verses have been used to judge and condemn our gay brothers and sisters and, as a result, cause a fracture in churches around the world—not around ethnic lines this time—but around sexual orientation.

I choose to believe that Paul's letter to the church in Rome worked—that it had the intended impact and harmonized the believers who were divided on issues of conscience and conviction. How much more beautiful, then, would it be if his words from two thousand years ago were similarly used today to help reconcile the church with the LGBTQ community. What a powerful reversal that would be of how his words have been used in the past.

May we one day be able to reimagine Paul's opening words in Romans 1:16:

> For I am not ashamed of the gospel, for it is the power of God for salvation to everyone who believes . . . to the straight, the gay, the lesbian, the bisexual, transgender, and queer.

CHAPTER 9

———————————➔

IMAGINE A CHURCH WHERE . . .

What's in a Name?

Naming your child is a big deal. At least it was for us.

Kate and I gravitate toward the more unique side of the spectrum when it comes to baby names. But as much as we loved what we came up with all four times, we didn't tell people what our boys' names were until after they were born. Here's why: if you tell someone what your child's unusual name is before they're born, they might make a strange face or feign excitement. But if you wait until they're *holding* the cute little ball of recently birthed squishiness, it doesn't matter what the name is. They're going to love it.

I wonder if that helps explain why we didn't name our church until almost two months in. By that time, the forty people who had jumped on board to join us in our adventure had already come to love the newly birthed community. I imagine we could have called it The Church of the Dancing Llamas and they would have thought it was the best name ever.[1]

Be that as it may, Kate, myself, Jessica, Mathew, Eric, and another Jessica—who constituted our early ministry team—had at last come up with a name we felt encapsulated the heartbeat of who we were trying to be in the world. And we couldn't wait to unveil it to everyone.

On the Saturday before Easter, in April 2014, we put together an all-day retreat for the whole church, designed to brainstorm ideas about what sort of faith community we could become. The plan was to reveal the new name at some point that day. So when Saturday came around, with most of the church in attendance, sitting under the arbor behind Larry and Cory's house, the bees were buzzing in nearby flowers and our people were buzzing with anticipation. After lunch, we all gathered back together so that Kate and I could share some of the driving values behind our dreams for the church. But everyone there was waiting, knowing we'd end our session by announcing the name.

At last the time had come. I turned to Kate, she smiled back at me. Not exactly like birthing a new child, but not entirely unlike it either. We held each other's gaze, savoring the moment. Amazed at where life had brought us.

Together we said, "The name of our church is . . ."

Similar Story, but Totally Different

Six weeks before that sunny day under the arbor, I had walked for the final time out of the church that brought us to San Diego. Despite our theological alignment, there was a clash of values around issues of leadership and the pastoral calling to shepherd people, as well as deep-seated patterns of unhealthiness that predated me and that I could not change. Kate and I tried to work out an exit plan for June so that our boys could finish the school year, but the elder board decided we should part ways in February, leaving us feeling stranded once again.

Looking back on both experiences, first in Arizona and then at the church in San Diego, there are some similarities, but the differences are what stand out. First, when you've already gone through a devastating loss and then see that there is life on the other side, it gives you strength to believe that you can rise again should you find yourself knocked out. Second, I was a more healthy and grounded person the second time around. I knew what I wanted and what I didn't want. I knew what was healthy and good for me and what wasn't. Third—and most important—I had an incredible, authentic, and loving community of friends who were there to carry me and my family.

I mentioned earlier that our friendships in Arizona could go only so deep, because relationships are built on connection, and connection happens only when we make ourselves known to people. Well, when we moved to San Diego and stepped into our newfound freedom, something amazing happened: we developed genuine friendships. For the first time, we could make ourselves known to others. I had never realized the power of authentic community before we moved to San Diego, when I no longer had to hide parts of who I was. So when we again stood on the outside looking in, we were met with the embrace of people who loved our family and who promised to take care of us no matter what happened.

I'm pleased to report they made good on those promises. Confirming what we already knew: these were gracious, generous, loving, genuine, quality people with whom we wanted to do life.

Relationships over a Bathtub and a Backyard

Unsure if we would stay in San Diego but also not ready to say goodbye to our community, Kate and I opened our house the Sunday following my abrupt end at our previous church for breakfast and coffee. Just as in Arizona, we chose to not put our story out there, to not tell anyone what happened or why I felt I could not remain on staff unless they reached out to us first. And this time around people *did* reach out. They lamented the decisions the church had made as they told us how they wouldn't be returning. So that Sunday morning, twenty-one people newly without a church home showed up at our house. We ate, drank, and talked for three hours while ten kids under the age of nine ran about. None of us knew what was next, but our connection to one another and our shared dream for a progressive faith community, where all people are loved, celebrated, and affirmed at the Table of Grace, drew us together.

When our friends left that afternoon, Kate and I were nourished by the time they spent in our house. However, we weren't yet certain what that meant. Our first inclination, as before, was to return to Oregon and see what, if any, opportunities were there. It wasn't so much that we *wanted* to go back, but we struggled to see how we could afford to stay in San Diego; and not just afford, but find a more suitable living situation for our family of six. Our house at the time was beginning to exact its toll on our family after three years. It had neither a bathtub nor a backyard, which I don't have tell you is not ideal for a family with four small boys.

But our friends had become our family. I have no shame in using such a cliché. And they, like us, were desperate for the unicorn church, yet had no options in San Diego. One by one they reached out to Kate and me to assure us that, if we stayed and wanted to start a new faith community, then we could count on their support: emotionally, physically, and financially.

Kate and I had first dreamed of planting a church back when we were in Arizona, when we were suffocating under the weight of being out of alignment. There was a stretch of time when we kept a notebook open, mapping out ideas, as they came to us, of what a faith community could look like. We would cuddle up on the couch, crowd around a laptop, and scout possible locations. I would reach out to different denominations and church-planting organizations, curious if anyone might be interested in partnering with us. In the end, though, we never felt the time was right.

On Thursday night, just four days after our twenty-one friends had been in our house to break bread, my wife and I stood in our kitchen running through all the possible scenarios, desperate for some direction, when finally it clicked. We were in a city we loved, surrounded by a small group of friends we loved even more, and they were ready and willing to leap with us. I have often said over the past couple of years that if you're starting a church and you're given the choice between a large sum of cash or a small group of kind and compassionate people, take the people every time.

"I choose relationships over a backyard and bathtub," Kate whispered that night.

Our eyes locked, like they did in the room with the floral patterns and the high ceilings, like they did before I walked in to the board meeting where I was fired, and like they did as we sat in the parking lot of Target. At those words, our decision had been made.

We were going to start a church together. As copastors . . . as equals.

Imagine a Church Where . . .

I've heard it said that life is about connection. We are here to be in relationship with one another. We *need* one another. I don't think the ancient Hebrew people were wrong when they taught that God created the world and said, "Those humans over there? Yeah, it's not good for them to be alone." Man or woman, gay or straight, black or white, young or old, religious or not—it doesn't matter. We are here for connection. Any movement to divide people, or keep people from being able to connect with others, is a fundamental move against the design and direction of creation.

In the kitchen that night we saw it: the invitation to provide a space where people can connect in meaningful ways that will lead them to love, life, and peace. This is what our life must be about, investing in relationships, in people. And we had such ideal soil for our new plant, with bubbling energy for an incredible running start; we knew we'd be foolish to pass up the opportunity.

So we began to imagine . . .

What would it look like to create a faith community where people learned to love themselves in a healthy way, which would free them up to love the people around them, all the while being grounded in the love of God?[2] We envisioned a place where people were honest about their flaws, their fears, and their doubts, and also about their hopes, their dreams, and what makes them come alive. A place where people could connect with one another by removing the masks we wear to protect ourselves, where we see other hurting people and say "me too"; a faith community that graciously holds space for all people, regardless of ethnicity, orientation, age, creed, or socioeconomic status. Where people would catch on to the idea that love is better than hate, that peace is better than war, that forgiveness is better than revenge, and that God is in the business of reconciling all things.

What would it look like to create a church where families could bring their children and trust that they wouldn't be indoctrinated into some religious system from which they'd one day need deprogramming? A church where parents could believe that their children would grow up knowing they are loved, cherished, accepted, valued, and celebrated for who they are. Where we would consciously push back against the shaming messages of the world like, "boys have to be tough," and "girls have to be quiet."

What would it look like to create a church where men and women served together, side by side, as equals? Where there was no single leader, but where leadership was shared? A church that was intentional about diffusing the pulpit power so that one person wasn't the sole mouthpiece for the whole body. Where space was given to hear from other voices, perspectives, feelings, and ideas. Where the sermon was not viewed as the most important event, but rather one possible element to curate a safe space for connection and worship.

What would it look like to create a church that was uniquely Christian, but not exclusively? Where we are compelled by the vision of the Kingdom of God on earth as it is in heaven, and where we orient our lives around the Way of Jesus, but don't pretend that Christianity is the sole arbiter of truth, goodness, or beauty?

What would it look like to create a church that wasn't *only* about LGBTQ inclusion but clearly was founded as an open and affirming church because they had earnestly studied the Bible and were determined to undo the damage done by its misuse?

What would it look like to create a church insistent that the world is in desperate need of a more just and generous expression of the Christian faith? Where the love and grace of God is allowed to freely flow and freely be received? Where the radical concept of inclusion and welcoming everybody suddenly is revealed to not be radical at all, but actually lays at the foundation of the gospel? A church where over and over again we insist that you are a loved child of God, fully welcome in the family?

Our imaginations ran wild at the possibilities.

The Table Is Set

So we invited everyone back the following Sunday. Come eat more homemade cranberry muffins and drink more single origin pour-over coffee, we said. Bring your kids if you have them, we said. And stay awhile, we insisted.

And they came, this time about thirty people. It was March 9, 2014, and Kate and I sat side by side as we looked at our friends crammed on our couches, sitting on carpets next to piles of crushed goldfish crackers, and knocking over picture frames as they leaned against our walls.

"We have decided we are going to stay in San Diego and start a new church. . . ." We barely got the words out before our friends, our *family*, started whooping and cheering, giving us an assortment of wry smiles as if to say, "It's cool, we've known the whole time, but it's nice to hear you two finally came around."

And so it began. From March to early June we met every Sunday in our living room, shoving the couches and dining room table against the walls to make space for everyone. There was steady growth, each week, as more people heard about what we were doing. True to our MO, we didn't call, text, or email anyone to invite them. We didn't post our intentions on Facebook or make a website. For three months, it was an underground movement, fueled only by word of mouth. People would show up at our living room on Sundays, eager to chase after the vision of a progressive Christian church and eager for authentic human connection.

By June there were fifty people showing up, and we no longer fit in our living room. A team was formed to hunt for venues—not an easy feat in urban San Diego. But we settled on an elementary school that would take us in, and that's where we've met for worship every week since.

If you show up early on a Sunday morning, you'll see us emptying our van full of furnishings as we transform the school's multipurpose room into a sacred space of engagement. We use rugs, lamps, candles, artwork, and soft fabrics in our attempt to maintain the vibe of our old living room. In the back is freshly brewed coffee and homemade food. You're invited to make yourself comfortable.

You might notice that the chairs are set up almost in the round, which at first feels jarring, because no matter where you sit someone can see you. And that's the point. We are not here to perform for you or to put on a show. This isn't a place where professional Christians do all the work and everyone else stares forward as consumers, like at a play or a movie. We realize you may feel like coming in and hiding, and we'll respect that, but know that when you're ready to be seen, we'll see you. And you can see us.

The band is off to the side, but not because they're no good. In fact, they're extremely talented musicians who volunteer hours of their time to curate an environment where people can connect to the Divine through music, prayer, and liturgy. We put them off to the side so that the focus is less on them and more on the content of the gathering.

When the service begins you might wonder, "When is everyone going to find their seats? Isn't this thing starting?" Trust us, we think that too sometimes. But eventually people will peel off from their conversations and make their way to chairs. Or they won't, which is fine. Then you might notice—no, scratch that, you will *absolutely* notice—that there are children, lots of them, everywhere. Some are up toward the front of the room, sitting or dancing or spinning in circles on the giant area rugs. Others are on their parents' laps or in their arms. Still more are in the back of the room trying to swipe a donut when no one is looking or are crowded around a table making art together. That's when you notice the art tables, and you smile. Because you, like us, know that not everyone expresses worship through music. So we put out tables and supplies, and we encourage people to make art throughout the gathering.

Depending on which Sunday you join us, who knows what might happen next. Some mornings we take turns striking a gong, causing the whole church to say, "What did *you* do?" Then the person who hit the gong shares with the whole church what they did during the week that they were proud of, and we all thunderously applaud them. Some mornings we listen as someone from the community shares a story about the formation, or transformation, of their faith. Some mornings we break off into small groups, scattered around the room, and spend time doing intentional (and at times, uncomfortable) activities designed to facilitate connection. Some mornings we do what we call Rock, Paper, Scissors Prayer, where everyone holds up one of the symbols depending on what they need prayer for: a rock means "relationships," paper means "work life," and scissors means "my inner self." Then we all pause, look around, and silently pray for one another. Some mornings we watch a video together, recite an ancient prayer, or participate in reading Scripture. Some mornings we have a sermon that artfully unpacks the Bible and engages the ancient stories with fresh eyes, and you'll notice how this progressive, inclusive vision of a more just and generous faith can come alive in powerful and transformative ways. Some mornings we ditch the sermon altogether and have an entire morning of interactive worship, with stations set up around the room: painting, writing, working with clay, and someone leading yoga in the corner. Some mornings, if we just wrapped up a sermon series, we forgo the sermon and spend time talking, as a group, about the past several weeks: What did you hear? What did you learn? What surprised you? What did you disagree with?

But every Sunday morning, no matter when you may come, we will always end our gathering by going to the Table, receiving the ancient symbols, the divine reminders that God is with us and God is for us. And we practice open Communion, so no matter who you are or where you come from, these gifts of grace are for you. All we ask is that you come with open hands, because in the words of my friend Stan, grace is not something we take, it is something we receive.

And then, when all is said and done, we close our gathering with the same ritual every week. It's how we've done it since we began in our living room, and we have no plans to stop. We all grab the hand of the person next to us and form one large circle—or amoeba, if necessary. But everyone is in. We are all connected. You are not alone.

Then, with hands held, someone will lead us in our benediction, the closing words that send us out into the week. We have just received the grace of God from the bread and the cup, and now we are sent to be the grace of God in the world. The benediction is the same every Sunday, so if you don't catch on the first time, it's okay. We'll do it again next week. They are words we borrowed from Glennon Doyle, because they speak so powerfully to the type of community we are building. It goes like this:

Leader: Be brave

All: Because you are a child of God

Leader: And be kind

All: Because so is everyone else

Then we all clap. Lots of people hug. Some have to leave right away, but you're welcome to stay as long as you'd like (or at least until 1:00 p.m., since that's as long as we've rented the school for). We'd love to have you join us next week, but it's okay if you don't. We are here, every Sunday, for those who need us; for those who need the weekly reminder that they are seen, they are loved, and they are enough.

And every Sunday since we began there have been new people, like you, who show up and wonder: Is it true? Does the unicorn church really exist?

We smile, understanding your delight mixed with skepticism, and we lead you to the Table and simply say, "It's true. And now that you're here, the feast can begin."

What's in a Name? Everything.

At our church, we hold space for one another and respect everyone's spiritual journey. The theological makeup of our community is as diverse as our ages, orientations, and ethnicities. Grace, freely given and freely received, flows between us as the only glue that can keep a group of ragamuffins and spiritual seekers like us together. We call one another out of our shame, and we sit with one another through the depths of our pain.

To put that more succinctly, we are a community of people who are being transformed in our spiritual journeys—assembled, strengthened, and maintained by God's grace—who bring all of our unique differences to the Table as we do life together.

Or, more succinctly still, and as Kate and I shared with our community that afternoon under the arbor, "We are called *Sojourn Grace Collective*."

Join us, won't you? There's room on the unicorn for everyone.

CHAPTER 10

REVISITING
FORGOTTEN WORDS

1 Corinthians 6:9 and 1 Timothy 1:10

At last we have reached our final chapter and our final two Clobber Passages. Up to this point we have UnClobbered Genesis 19 (a story of gang rape and inhospitality), Leviticus 18 and 20 (priestly restrictions against blurring the boundaries of Israelite identity), and Romans 1 (a passage intended to expose Jewish prejudice and reconcile the Roman church). There are two passages left that have traditionally been used to condemn homosexuality and exclude the LGBTQ community from full participation in the life of the church: 1 Corinthians 6:9 and 1 Timothy 1:10.

My experience has been that these two verses are the most utilized Clobber Passages, likely because the majority of English translations use (erroneously, as we'll soon see) the terms *homosexuality* or *homosexual*, making them easy to find and easy to misuse. I think back to the week after

I was fired from my church in Arizona, when I first dealt with people criticizing me for "not reading my Bible."

All You Need Is Google

As word began to spread about my termination, more than one well-intentioned person tried to save me from my heretical ways. And, of course, Facebook was the logical battleground—the place where minds are changed about as often as the Cubs win the World Series.[1] Their weapon of choice? The almighty meme; not just any meme, these were special, with clever backgrounds overlaid by bold Bible verses. I think one might have even had a cat on it.

So imagine it's fall 2011, you are a non-affirming Christian at my church, and you just discovered that I was fired because of my inclusive theology on homosexuality. Since our church had never taught on the subject or had any discussion on it, you realize you don't even know *why* you believe homosexuality is wrong. You just know. But now one of your pastors has been fired over it.

"Wait," you say to yourself, "isn't the Bible clear? It's obviously against homosexuality, right?"

Yet a sliver of doubt creeps across the threshold of your mind because you also felt like you trusted and respected me. So in a moment of confusion and bewilderment you do what all people do when faced with the unknown . . .

You ask Siri.

"Siri," you whisper, hoping no one hears you from the other room, "what does the Bible say about homosexuality?"

Google god strikes up the band of little elves and sends them coursing through countless articles and blogs, finding the best matches for "Bible" and "homosexuality." Thanks to modern English translators, these elves waste no time in finding precisely what you're looking for.

"Mr. Jones," Siri responds, in a sexy British accent (because who *hasn't* changed their Siri to this?), "I've found the following answers to your question."

You look, and your phone is littered with links to 1 Corinthians 6:9–10 (ESV), which reads, "Do not be deceived . . . [no] men who practice homosexuality . . . will inherit the kingdom of God."

"Phew," you sigh in relief, "okay good, the Bible *does* condemn homosexuality. Just like I thought . . . er, hoped . . . er, assumed. Sheesh," you think to yourself, "that was easy. Strange that Colby didn't . . ."

And then it hits you.

Maybe Colby has never read this verse before. Maybe all this could have been avoided if he just read 1 Corinthians 6:9. It's so clear and obvious. "Perhaps it's not too late!" you exclaim.

So you find a fancy meme with 1 Corinthians 6:9 layered over a picturesque mountaintop, copy the URL, hop over to my Facebook wall, and paste it with a mix of pride and enthusiasm. You sit back and wait for the red bubble notifying you that I "liked" it, trusting I will thank you in due time.

I wish I could say the above scenario was a bit of creative fiction, but it happened . . . more times than I care to admit.

People were convinced that I somehow must have missed this Clobber Passage from 1 Corinthians, misused by so many Christians to deny LGBTQ people their rightful place in the Kingdom of God.

Far from having missed it, I pored over it, as I did every other Clobber Passage, desperate to know what the writers of Scripture really said and really meant. Instead of condemning homosexuality, I believe Paul, in these final two passages, lays groundwork for creating healthy sexual boundaries for all people. So now, I want to end by proposing that God is calling all of us—gay, straight, bisexual, transgender, queer—out of places of guilt and shame and into a place of wholehearted, integrated living where we are rooted in God's love for us and committed to loving ourselves and our neighbor *even when it comes to our sexual activities*. If, at the end of rethinking our misuse of the Bible on homosexuality, we can reasonably and confidently proclaim that the Clobber Passages do not, in fact, condemn our gay siblings or prohibit a same-sex couple from fully thriving in a relationship blessed by God, then what is left for the church to do toward the LGBTQ community but humble ourselves, acknowledge our sin of denying them a seat at the Table, and welcome them with open arms to be full participants in our churches.

But before we turn to the verses at hand, we need to reconsider the common mistake of reducing the complexity of these Clobber Passages (and at times, this topic in general) down to one overly simplistic question. I find this question to be unhelpful—if not downright irrelevant—in the pursuit of a thoughtful critique of the Clobber Passages found in 1 Corinthians 6 and 1 Timothy 1.

Is Homosexuality a Sin?

Remember the question I was asked right out of the gate in my inquisition with the board: "Do you think homosexuality is a sin?" I find this an odd question for a couple of reasons.

First, even though the term *homosexuality* encompasses more than just what people do in their beds, what I've found is that when someone asks this question, what they *mean* is, "Do you think gay sex is a sin?" Therefore, if a person believes that sex between two men or two women is sinful, then the answer for them becomes a simple, "Yes, homosexuality is a sin."

Second, I've also found that my inability to give what the inquirer assumes should be a simple yes or no answer frustrates both them and me. Let me explain.

Once again, imagine that you are a non-affirming Christian who is convinced the Bible condemns homosexuality. We're hanging out, watching Monday Night Football, and the subject of sexuality comes up. You don't know me that well, so you ask if I think homosexuality is a sin. I noticeably hem and haw, while nursing my pint of Belgian Ale, and you sense I'm about to monologue. You snort a little and tell me, "It's a simple question, yes or no?"

I pause and look up at a screen, pretending to check on the score, "Well, answer me this . . . do you think premarital sex is a sin?"

"Yes," you reply, "I do." You follow up by acknowledging that some Christians feel otherwise, but for you the sacredness of sex is reserved only for a man and woman in the context of marriage.

Then I ask you, "How about if I, as a married straight man, had an affair with another woman?" You roll your eyes. "Of course that's a sin!"

I quickly follow up with, "Or what if, instead of an affair, I visited a strip club? Or maybe slept with a prostitute?"

You were in mid-sip at this point, and at the mention of "prostitute" you nearly spit your ale out. "Come on," you shout, annoyed at me, "are you genuinely questioning me about the sinfulness of soliciting prostitutes? What are you getting at?"

I smile, enjoying myself, "Okay, just to be clear though, sex with my own wife . . . sinful or no?"

"No," you retort. "Like I said—in the confines of the marriage covenant, consensual sex between a man and a woman is a beautiful—and non-sinful—gift of God."

"Thanks for your honesty. So then, I have just one more question. . . . Is heterosexuality a sin?"

"Well," you set your glass down, narrow your eyes, and tilt your head to the side, slow to respond, "I guess sometimes yes and sometimes no."

Sometimes Yes, Sometimes No

We may not all agree on the criteria, but most Christians take as a given the space to parse out when heterosexual sex is a sin and when it's not. As a result, giving a one-word answer to the question, "Is *heterosexuality* a sin?" is neither practical nor helpful. Nuance is demanded.

Given the Bible's lack of condemnation thus far (the present two Clobber Passages notwithstanding, although they shan't be standing much longer), I'm suggesting the same space be given for the "sometimes yes, sometimes no" position for homosexual activities. If you think about it, this squares rather well with what we've discovered so far in our study of the Clobber Passages. From a biblical perspective, we would be in safe territory, for instance, to suggest that same-sex rape, same-sex prostitution, same-sex worship orgies, and same-sex adultery could fall into the "yes, that's sinful" category.

I believe it is possible to be an open and affirming Christian while also holding fast to scriptural values and principles regarding sexual morality. I'm not proposing that we ditch verses we dislike or that don't fit in our desired worldview. Nor am I suggesting we turn to LGBTQ individuals and give them carte blanche to follow any and all of their desires. Instead, I'm hoping we can find a place, guided by the Spirit and Scripture, where all people, regardless of orientation, are invited to enjoy *some* expressions of sexual intimacy and avoid others.

But that proposition will be valid only if, indeed, I'm correct, and we need to rethink how we have understood, and misused, these final two Clobber Passages.

Small Difference, Significant Consequence

When I was ten years old, my mom lost her sense of good judgment. Evidently my skills at making grilled cheese sandwiches and Top Ramen had convinced her that I was ready to bake the apple pie for Thanksgiving.[2] Now, it *might* have been a tolerable tasting pie were it not for one minor mistranslation in the recipe. To this eager ten-year-old, 3 "tsp" of salt and 3 "tbs" of salt were easily confused. So when my precious Thanksgiving pie showed up at our family gathering, baked by a proud, chubby preteen whose previous culinary masterpiece consisted of cheesy scrambled eggs atop Wonder Bread toast, no one saw it coming.

Two words from two of Paul's letters have likewise suffered mistranslations that have led to significant consequences and ensuing misuse—albeit far more damaging and impactful than a regurgitated bite of pie-flavored salt.

The first word is *malakoi*, and it's found in 1 Corinthians 6:9. The second word, *arsenokoitai*, shows up twice: directly after *malakoi* in Corinthians and then again in 1 Timothy 1:10:

> Or do you not know that the unrighteous will not inherit the kingdom of God? Do not be deceived; neither fornicators, nor idolaters, nor adulterers, nor effeminate [*malakoi*], nor homosexuals [*arsenokoitai*], nor thieves, nor the covetous, nor drunkards, nor revilers, nor swindlers, will inherit the kingdom of God. Such were some of you; but you were washed, but you were sanctified, but you were justified in the name of the Lord Jesus Christ and in the Spirit of our God. (1 Cor. 6:9–11 NASB)

And . . .

> But we know that the Law is good, if one uses it lawfully, realizing the fact that law is not made for a righteous person, but for those who are lawless and rebellious, for the ungodly and sinners, for the unholy and profane, for those who kill their fathers or mothers, for murderers and immoral men and homosexuals [*arsenokoitai*] and kidnappers and liars and perjurers, and whatever else is contrary to sound teaching. (1 Tim. 1:8–10 NASB)

Throughout the last few centuries, translators have failed to reach consensus on how to handle these two words.

A quick sampling of how *malakoi* and *arsenokoitai* have been translated respectively:

— effeminate; abusers of themselves with mankind (KJV)
— male prostitutes; practicing homosexuals (NIV)
— men who practice homosexuality (ESV combined the two words)

The implications for how to apply Paul's words depends on which direction the translators went. Do these words describe who people *are* or what they *do?* Words such as *effeminate* and *homosexual* are about a person's identity. Words such as *prostitute* and *men who practice homosexuality* refer to actions. So imagine an eleven-year-old boy, struggling to understand his blossoming feelings for other boys his age, walking to his grandmother's shelf to pick up a Bible. If he is unfortunate enough to grab an NASB or an NKJV, then he'll discover that simply *having* these feelings will exclude him from the Kingdom of God. However, if his heritage favors the NIV or the ESV, at least he'll find comfort in the idea that he'll only be sinning if he *acts* on these desires.

We can do better. For the sake of children now, and for the untold millions of adults who grew up with conflicting and damaging messages, we *have* to do better.

So, is Paul telling the church in Corinth and his compatriot Timothy that men who are born with same-sex attraction are unrighteous and destitute sinners? Or is he saying that if men engage in same-sex sex acts then they will be guilty of lawlessness?

Or might he be saying something else altogether?

Lost in Translation

Translation between any two languages is a tricky and nuanced business. It's rare to find an exact word-for-word translation that encompasses the full meaning and nuance of each respective language. Difficulties arise, for example, when trying to translate a word from a visual language to a technical one. When it comes to the Bible, there are even more layers of complications and anxiety because no one wants to mishandle sacred texts that we believe were inspired by God and that have been preserved and handed down for several millennia.

All that is to say, I have deep respect and high regard for the men and women who have labored over the centuries to translate the Bible into various languages. And yet . . . the words *homosexuals* and *homosexuality* have zero business being in the Bible.

Whatever we think about Paul's two Greek words, we need to be better disciplined than to use clinical terms that entered the English lexicon one hundred fifty years ago and that carry with them all sorts of cultural assumptions and baggage. To be a homosexual, according to today's understanding, is to identify with a subset of the population who experience an enduring pattern of emotional, romantic, and/or sexual attractions to members of the same sex.[3]

Who we experience these attractions toward—be it members of the opposite sex (heterosexuality), the same sex (homosexuality), or either sex (bisexuality)—is not something we make a conscious choice about. We are born, in some way, shape, or form, with these patterns, even if the patterns might also be shaped in various ways by how we are raised.

The concept of sexual orientation is complex and evolving. How we think about it and understand it today is nuanced and intricate. It is also categorically different from how ancient civilizations thought about it. And so my point is that it is anachronistic to use a nineteenth-century clinical term, ripe with modern meaning, confusion, and implications, when translating words from a culture unlike our own from two thousand years ago.

At least for the first few hundred years of English translation, these two words were translated to describe a type of sexual perversion between two men. It was believed Paul was referencing actions, not identity. Yet, over the past century, with the advent of awareness around orientation as an inborn aspect of one's identity, the translations shifted to using terms that condemn men for simply being who they are.

You can understand, then, the importance of rethinking our misuse of these Clobber Passages.

Before I move on to the two words in question, my goal is not to prove that one translation of a text is the "correct" translation. I am not presuming to have the definitive statement on the issue. Rather, I want to show how a faithful reading of the text, in its historical and textual context, can lead to an interpretation that is just as plausible—if not more so—than how the church has historically understood them.

With that in mind, let's listen in as Paul warns both the church in Corinth and his friend Timothy about certain vices that prohibit someone from life in God's Kingdom.

Soft

A brief outline of 1 Corinthians 5–7 will show how the Clobber Passage sits in a bigger argument that culminates with a condemning word toward having sex with prostitutes.

Paul, beginning the discussion of what is and is not appropriate sexual conduct, launches chapter 5 by condemning a man in the church for sleeping with his father's wife (i.e., his stepmother). He then moves through chapter 6 by expressing disgust that the church is seeking outside legal counsel to deal with economic internal affairs (they were suing one another) and reminds the church of how they used to conduct themselves (which is where the Clobber Passage sits, in a list of vices in verses 9 and 10).

Finally, he returns to sexual conduct by reminding them that their bodies are temples of God, and if they sleep around (like, with prostitutes), they join their bodies (and hence, Christ's body) to others. Paul wraps up in chapter 7 by taking the church back to middle school via basic Sex Ed 101, describing marriage, celibacy, and abstinence.

So the flow goes like this: sexual immorality, then financial exploitation, and ending with sexual immorality *combined* with exploitation. These two themes are intertwined, and that's key to understanding what Paul might have been talking about in our Clobber Passage.

First, let's look at *malakoi*, which appears in a vice list in chapter 6.

> Or do you not know that the unrighteous will not inherit the kingdom of God? Do not be deceived; neither fornicators, nor idolaters, nor adulterers, nor [*malakoi*], nor [*arsenokoitai*]. (1 Cor. 6:9 NASB)

The word *malakoi* was used in three ways. In its most basic form, *malakoi* simply means "soft." In fact, in two other places, the New Testament uses *malakoi* to describe soft fabric. That's simple enough. Second, beyond the literal usage, *malakoi* was used in a moral context to describe someone who was spineless. Perhaps the person was lazy or lacked self-control, had a soft disposition. The person was weak.

The third way *malakoi* was used was in a pejorative sense to describe a "womanly man," clearly a disgrace in a male-dominated patriarchal society. This goes beyond someone being weak-willed and moves into describing the person as being "like a woman," which was seen as even worse. This is why some translators go with "effeminate," to communicate this idea of being unmanly.

In a sexual context (as Paul used it in his list of vices), *malakoi* could therefore be understood as the passive partner in a sexual encounter. The one assuming, if you will, the "feminine" position. This is why some translators see this as a phrase to describe male prostitution.

Pertinent to this discussion is that in Paul's time it was not uncommon for married, heterosexual men to have an erotic relationship with a young boy on the side. Far from being an expression of a person's orientation, however, this was about pleasure, excess, and even (on some twisted level) a way for an upper-class person to pass on the ways of culture to the next generation. The ancients referred to this as "pederasty." Though this practice was widely accepted in the ancient world, by the time of Paul, growing numbers of philosophers and moralists criticized sexual intercourse within the pederastic relationship.

My point in bringing this up is twofold: first, to avoid the pitfall that some well-meaning interpreters have succumbed to when attempting to UnClobber these verses. Sometimes it is suggested that Paul is condemning pederasty when he uses *malakoi* and *arsenokoitai*. But it seems to me that he would have used language readily available to him, such as *paiderastia*, a compound word describing the erotic love of children (specifically boys).

Second, even though I don't think Paul was targeting pederasty (although I have no doubt that he would have condemned it if asked), I still get the sense that echoes of the pederastic relationship would have been in the Corinthians minds when Paul used words like *malakoi* and *arsenokoitai*. Pederasty, at its core, was an extreme combination of sexual immorality and exploitation; not dissimilar to prostitution, and not dissimilar to the activities Paul was describing with *malakoi* and *arsenokoitai*.

In other words, what I suggest Paul condemned with his use of *malakoi* and—as we'll see—*arsenokoitai* in his vice list, were same-sex sex acts that were exploitive and transactional. He invited the Corinthian church to embody a community that was holy, set apart from the culture around them, similar to how Levitical Law called Israel to not commit *toevah*. This separation of licentious behavior would have been crucial to Paul's church-planting experiment, especially in a city like Corinth, a hotbed of egregious fornication.

No, says Paul, they were to be different. God, through Jesus, was calling them to a better and new way of living:

One where people don't solicit for sex;

One where people don't treat their bodies as a commodity;

One where people don't treat others' bodies as a commodity;

One where people are respected and honored, not used as property;

One where people do not use power and privilege to take advantage of those below them.

I Do Not Think It Means
What You Think It Means

The second word in this Clobber Passage, *arsenokoitai*, is sometimes translated "homosexuals," or "men who practice homosexuality."

These, I'd like to say again, are modern terms that should not be in the Bible.

But they are. And as a result, a lot of people have been told they have no shot at life in God's Kingdom, while others received a false sense of confidence that they are standing on solid, biblical ground in excluding the LGBTQ community. But if *arsenokoitai* doesn't mean "people born with same-sex attraction," or even, "men who engage in any and all same-sex sex acts," then what does it mean?

Great question.

Truth be told, no one knows.

You see, it's not like most other Greek words, which we can compare against other usages during that time to find out how people used it and what it meant to them. Instead, *arsenokoitai*, a compound word of *arsen* (meaning "male") and *koite* (meaning "bed) seems to be a word that Paul might have made up. Scholars conjecture that Paul created a compound word from how the Septuagint (the Greek translation of the Hebrew Old Testament) translated Leviticus 18:22 and 20:13, which used both *arsenos* and *koiten*.

That makes sense. But what I disagree with is the assumption that Paul intended to condemn *all* conceivable expressions of homosexuality. I've already demonstrated how Leviticus was not a blanket condemnation against any and all same-sex sex acts. Therefore, if Paul was indeed drawing from those verses, it does not tell us *more* than that. It likely doesn't tell us less, either. Meaning, there's no doubt Paul was speaking to sexual activity between two men. Yet, just as Leviticus had no word against people born with same-sex attraction, nor a same-sex couple in a loving, committed relationship, neither did Paul.

So what might Paul have been speaking against? What activity, in addition to participating in swindling, idolatry, and committing adultery, will exclude a person from inheriting the Kingdom of God? I believe Paul had in mind a specific exploitive expression of same-sex sex acts. This is altogether different than saying Paul was condemning any and all sexual activity between two men.

Paul may have coined, or at least been an early user of, *arsenokoitai*, but it does show up in other documents not long after Paul. And when it does, it is used in contexts where the author was addressing economic or exploitive concerns—sometimes with zero mention of sexual activity. The few times it is used in a context of sex acts, it is juxtaposed with economic and exploitive language—just as it is in our Clobber Passages:

> Neither the sexually immoral nor idolaters nor adulterers nor male prostitutes [*malakoi*] nor homosexual offenders [*arsenokoitai*] nor thieves nor the greedy. . . ." (1 Cor. 6:9 NIV 1984)

"the sexually immoral, men who practice homosexuality [*arsenokoitai*], enslavers, liars, perjurers . . ." (1 Tim. 1:10 ESV)

Notice the progression from sexual immorality in general, to *malakoi* and *arsenokoitai*, and then to economic exploitation and immorality.

So at the risk of being a broken record, was Paul condemning people born with same-sex attraction? No. Was he condemning any and all same-sex sex acts? No. Was he condemning sexual activity, engaged in by people of the same sex, that was either exploitive (such as pederasty) or economic (such as prostitution) in nature? It would sure seem so.

So then, is it reasonable to suggest that he is therefore *endorsing* same-sex marriage or even a loving, committed, mutual same-sex relationship? Of course not! That would be overstepping the scope of Paul's argument. Paul's lack of condemnation is not equivalent to an endorsement. But we do need to be honest about the existence of a "sometimes yes" category for when same-sex sex acts were considered sinful by Paul.

Consistency across the Board

To recap, if *malakoi* was Paul's way of talking about the "soft" men who were making themselves available for sexual exploitation, then *arsenokoitai* would have covered those who were engaging in same-sex prostitution and exploiting others in a sexual way.

What it appears Paul is saying is that people who are *malakoi* and *arsenokoitai*, who see others as less than, who abuse their power and privilege, who sell themselves in prostitution or who engage in prostitution and the degrading of the lower classes, those people are like adulterers, fornicators, idolaters, thieves, and greedy slave owners.

They are not part of what God is doing through Jesus. They are not part of the Kingdom of God.

This resonates well with the consistency we discussed at the beginning of the chapter, holding space for the "sometimes yes, sometimes no" dynamic of both heterosexuality and homosexuality.

Now, it would be a mistake to read Paul and think, "He is writing these verses to clarify how some expressions of same-sex activity are out of keeping with a Kingdom ethic, but others he would have been fine with." In other words, while I am arguing that we hold space for a nuanced "sometimes yes, sometimes no" posture of sinfulness when it comes to heterosexual sex *and* homosexual sex, I can't imagine that would have been Paul's posture. I say that, because for Paul and the rest of the ancient world, there was no concept of a person's sexual orientation, as I've already mentioned; envisioning a "sometimes not sinful" posture for a same-sex couple would have been beyond the consciousness of humanity in the first century. If I had a time machine and could send any of my friends from our church who are in a loving, committed, same-sex relationship to meet Paul and ask him what he thought, the only mental categories Paul had, the only boxes he would put them in, would resemble a pederastic or a prostitution-like relationship, with one partner in the dominant, exploitative role. My friends could try all they want to plead their case to the contrary. They could swipe through wedding photos on their phone and tell tales from their dating years. They could explain how they enjoy long talks into the night, binge watching *Orange Is the New Black*, walking on the beach hand in hand, and laughing together at *Bad Lip Reading* videos. But as they recount their experiences of intimacy within the context of mutuality, Paul wouldn't have ears to hear it, and we can't fault him for that. There was no box for the category of a loving, committed, mutually respecting (and nonexploitive) same-sex relationship.

What we can do, and what we ought to do, is try and understand the specific types of sexual activity (both heterosexual and homosexual) that Paul identified as *not* representative of the new thing God was doing in the world through Jesus. This included activities like keeping young boys as sex-slaves, engaging in prostitution, and participating in pagan idol-worship orgies. I don't think any reasonable, thinking Christian would argue against the immorality of such endeavors.

So it seems to me that if we would understand Paul's words in this way, then we could find some common ground across the spectrum of Christian churches. There could be great unity of heart and mind about what, according to Paul, are sex-acts that are not representative of God's Kingdom, that are not beneficial to the work of Spirit in us, and that keep us enslaved to the powers of sin and death.

Having said that, what has happened instead is we've created categories for heterosexual people for what is acceptable and what isn't, but we've rejected such possibilities for those born with same-sex attraction. What I propose is that we can still be biblical, with a high view of Scripture, *and* affirm our gay and lesbian siblings.

Imagine what the church could look like and what our culture could look like, if boys and girls grew up knowing that, whatever their sexual orientation, we are all in this together.

There aren't separate rules, expectations, and allowances for one group but not the other.

If you're straight, don't be flippant with your body.

Don't treat it as if it has no value.

Don't break your covenants.

Don't cheat on people.

Don't sell yourself, and don't devalue others by treating them like a commodity.

Don't use your power or influence to take advantage of others.

Likewise, if you're gay, lesbian, bisexual, transgender, or queer, don't be flippant with your body.

Don't treat it as if it has no value.

Don't break your covenants.

Don't cheat on people.

Don't sell yourself, and don't devalue others by treating them like a commodity.

Don't use your power or influence to take advantage of others.

To pursue a life oriented around the Kingdom of God with regard to sex should look the same for everyone.

Something's Still Missing

Before closing this chapter, I want to say a word about eunuchs. Most often, a eunuch in the ancient world was a castrated male. This meant they could work in the royal palace and not be a threat to the princess and the queen, or to the king's harem. However, less commonly known, is that the Hebrew word *saris*, which is often translated as "eunuch," was used in a far broader sense. It was a generic word that referred to those who *would* not or *could* not produce offspring, who were physically, mentally, or in any other way unable or unwilling to procreate. In other words, eunuchs were men who were either (a) castrated, (b) not aroused by women, or (c) men who chose celibacy.

Consider the following observations about eunuchs in the ancient world.

There were slave-trading laws in ancient Rome that allowed buyers to return their "purchase" if it was flawed. In defining the specifics of the return policy, there was a distinction between two types of eunuchs: a natural eunuch or a man-made eunuch. A man-made eunuch was referred to as a diseased male who was missing body parts, that is, a castrated male. A natural eunuch, however, was considered non-defective—meaning he was anatomically whole and procreation was biologically unimpeded—but it was described as psychologically difficult.

Pliny the Elder, a first-century Roman philosopher, referred to eunuchs as the "third gender, called half-male."[4] According to Pliny, this included men whose testicles were destroyed by either injury (castration, man-made) or by natural causes.

Some rabbis in ancient Judaism, acknowledging different types of eunuchs, believed that the "natural eunuch" could be cured. Others asserted that such men should simply remain celibate: "Some men by birth have a nature to turn away from women, and those who are subjected to this natural constitution do well not to marry."[5]

In the fourth century, Christian theologian Gregory of Nazianzus warned natural eunuchs not to be proud about their self-restraint toward women. A natural eunuch not desiring a woman is, well, *natural*, according to Gregory. He explains that "fire naturally burns, snow is naturally cold, and the sun by nature shines. Yet neither fire, snow, nor sun boast."[6] My point is this: the reality that not all people are born with an innate attraction to the opposite sex is as old as the human race. Ancient people were aware of this phenomenon even if they didn't have all the modern resources we have now to articulate, classify, study, and categorize it. But what they *did* was describe some men as natural-born eunuchs. They recognized that, while these men had all the proper anatomical features of a male, they were nonetheless not sexually aroused by women. If these same men were alive today, with our vernacular and understanding, they would likely identify as gay.

This tells me that if Paul's ultimate intent in these final two Clobber Passages was to make a blanket condemnation of men who were not attracted to women, he actually had language to do so. You could, for example, imagine him speaking out against the desires of the natural eunuch as a way to prohibit such behavior or relationships from participation in the Kingdom.

That alone is interesting to me, but when you further consider Jesus' words in Matthew 19, as well as the story of Philip and the Ethiopian eunuch in Acts 8, a larger picture emerges.

In Matthew 19, Jesus was engaged in a dialogue with Pharisees about divorce and remarriage. After his disciples moaned about the difficulty of Jesus' teaching, they said, "If that's the case, then it is better not to even marry!" To which Jesus responded with,

> "Not everyone can accept this word, but only those to whom it has been given. For there are eunuchs who were born that way, and there are eunuchs who have been made eunuchs by others—and there are those who choose to live like eunuchs for the sake of the kingdom of heaven. The one who can accept this should accept it." (Matt. 19:11–12 NIV)

We can assume that Jesus was well aware that the term *eunuch* applied to both males who were castrated (man-made) and those who had no inclination toward women (natural). His usage of it was no accident, and he seems well aware of the difficulty of his teaching. Jesus affirmed the ancient understanding of the different types of eunuchs, yet, just as with Paul, he offered no words of condemnation against the men (or their desires) who were born with no sexual attraction toward women.

Strikingly, what we do find is a barrier-shattering story in Acts 8. The Kingdom of God, inaugurated in the life of Jesus, vindicated and initiated in his death and resurrection, is now being implemented by God's Spirit through the early church at a rapid rate. Included in the implementation are moments, one right after another, where the early church has to come to grips with the inclusivity of the gospel. They are forced to see that the Kingdom is open for everyone.

Philip, following the leading of God's Spirit, finds himself in the presence of a eunuch from Ethiopia. Whether man-made or natural-born, we do not know. But I don't think that's the point. The point is that this new thing that God is doing through Jesus has broken through the wall of the sexual "other," a category of people that were previously outsiders from a Jewish perspective. Yet now, through the witness of Philip, a eunuch has come into relationship with God through Jesus Christ and given the gift of baptism. He joins the rest of the family at the Table . . . with zero words of condemnation.

So, Is Homosexuality a Sin?

I started this chapter by pushing back against the notion that it's a simple yes or no to the question, "Is homosexuality a sin?"

What we've discovered, by revisiting the final two Clobber Passages and through a deeper understanding of eunuchs, is that the Bible makes no effort to condemn those who are born with same-sex attraction. Nor does it have any word against loving, committed, mutually respecting relationships between people of the same sex.

What it *does* make an effort to condemn is contextually specific sexual activity between two men. And just as in Leviticus, we are reminded how women are not mentioned at all, further casting doubt that the Bible stands against homosexuality. In these Clobber Passages, Paul calls out *malakoi* and *arsenokoitai* as sexual activities that do not align with the mission of implementing the Kingdom of God on earth as it is in heaven.

The most reasonable explanation for what Paul meant in 1 Corinthians 6 and 1 Timothy 1 is not a blanket condemnation of any and all same-sex sex acts but condemnation of acts that were exploitive in nature, such as prostitution, seduction, or pederastic-type relationships.

Thus concludes our rethinking of our misuse of the Bible on homosexuality.

So, where does it leave us? Well, I imagine that depends on where you started from when you picked up this book.

If you came to *UnClobber* torn by the tension between your head and your heart, desiring a more open and expansive posture toward the gay community but feeling restricted because you believed the Bible condemned homosexuality and same-sex relationships, then you are in an exciting place, my friend. Hopefully, at this point, you have been liberated from such beliefs. The Clobber Passages do not teach what you thought they did.

If you came to *UnClobber* convinced that the church has been wrong in its treatment toward LGBTQ people but never knew what to do with the Bible, then I hope this book has brought you resolution. You need not discard the Bible in your pursuit of a more open and affirming faith.

If you came to *UnClobber* skeptical that a formerly conservative evangelical Christian pastor can believe as I do and still have a thriving ministry grounded in the gospel, then I hope I've been able to scratch away a portion of your skepticism.

Finally, and for me *most exciting,* if you came to *UnClobber* desperate to know if you can be both gay/lesbian/bisexual/transgender/queer *and* a Christian who holds the Scriptures in high regard, then know that I have overflowing joy for the road ahead of you—you beautiful, loved, child of God, you. Close this book, think of a friend or family member to pass it on to, and step out into the light. Recall the words of our Savior, who liberated the woman manipulated and used by the stone-throwing men in John 8:10–11:

> "Woman, where are they? Is there no one to condemn you?"
> She said, "No one, sir."
> Jesus said, "Neither do I condemn you."

Where are the verses that condemn you, oh child of God? Oh, what's that? There are none? Incredible! Then neither does the Lord.

As for me, where I'm at, there is nothing but hope-filled possibilities in front us. The landscape of Christianity in America (and the world) is evolving toward a more just, generous, and open expression of God's love and grace. Though there may not be enough unicorn churches like Sojourn Grace, that is changing as we speak. Walls are coming down. Bridges are being built. I *would* say that the Table is expanding, but the reality is that the Table has *always* been expansive. It's bigger than we could ever dream or imagine. There are just more and more of us waking up to this truth.

When it comes to homosexuality in the Bible, after revisiting the Clobber Passages, I'm convinced it is impossible to argue that the Bible condemns homosexuality as an orientation or that it divinely prohibits two people of the same sex from experiencing a loving, committed, mutually honoring and respecting relationship. In fact, the most a non-affirming Christian could say against people who identify as LGBTQ would be something like this: the Bible condemns gang rape, sexual molestation, religious orgies, prostitution, sex slaves, and exploiting people for sex.

To which we would all say . . .

Amen.

EPILOGUE

———————————→

AS YOU GO IN YOUR JOURNEY

The Life of the Ages

Years ago I was cruising down the path of a conservative evangelical view of Christianity. Part of what that meant was I believed that homosexuality was a sin and that gay people were sinners. Like so many others, I assumed the Bible was clear on such matters.

Then I hit an abrupt wall on my path when confronted with what it meant, in practical terms, to hold such beliefs: LGBTQ individuals were cast aside, prevented from full participation in the body of Christ. This realization exposed a tension between what I believed in my head and what I felt in my heart. It revealed that I was out of alignment.

So I studied the Clobber Passages and discovered that we had been misusing the Bible when it comes to homosexuality. To the relief of my soul, my head and heart at last found alignment. Yet finding alignment in that one area caused a greater reality to surface: I was not integrated as a pastor in my church. The call of God on my life was to find wholeness, to live on the outside what I believed on the inside. It was a painful process and included ammunition for lots of reasons to give up on the church and give up on my vision of pastoring people. Through the grace of God, the love of my wife, and the support of family and friends, I kept going. When the world says "give up," hope whispers "try it one more time."

As a result of finding personal and professional alignment and inviting others to find it along with me, an unbelievable quality of fruit has been produced in my life and in our faith community. It continues to blow my mind.

And yet it shouldn't, right? If I understand Jesus correctly, we are simply experiencing what he called the Abundant Life, the Life of the Ages, Eternal Life—pick your translation.

As You Go from Here

My hope with *UnClobber* was twofold. First, I wanted to reveal a faithful reading of the Clobber Passages that debunks, or at least diminishes, the certainty of the traditional perspective that the Bible is anti-gay. Second, I wanted to tell a story about transformation, alignment, and wholeness.

For some of you, this book will be the beginning of your journey. Perhaps for the first time you can imagine a more just and generous Christian faith, fully welcoming, affirming, and inclusive of the LGBTQ community. And now that you have been unchained from a view of the Bible that prohibited you from opening your hearts to your gay friends and family, you are ready to start moving forward in greater love, grace, and acceptance.

For others, this book is an affirmation of the journey you are already on, and it's a breath of fresh air to know that you are not alone. But maybe my story will give you a nudge to move into a more public and vocal support of the LGBTQ community. Perhaps you find yourself in a situation similar to where I was, in a place where you feel you have to keep your convictions close to your chest. I hope you are inspired to step into the light, find alignment, and discover the gifts awaiting you.

Still others of you might not know what implications this book will have for your journey, but if you're reading this, then it probably means you made it through all ten chapters. So I say, well done. I know the courage it must have taken you to do so. And I thank you for being open to listening to different perspectives and for letting me tell my story.

For the progressive Christian who has been wounded by the church and by Christians, I pray you see those who hurt you as Christ saw the Roman soldiers, and say, "Forgive them, for they know not what they do." For the conservative Christian who remains convinced that homosexuality is not God's design and that same-sex relationships are not okay, I pray you see the LGBTQ community not as people to fix or sinners to shun but as fellow humans created in the image of God to love, listen to, and seek to understand. For those struggling to know what they believe in all this or wondering how (or if) to follow the small voices in their hearts that might be calling them to frightening new places, I pray you let go of the need for certainty and lean in to trust that God is the Author and Perfecter of your faith.

No matter who you are or what journey you are on, know this: *you are a loved and fully accepted child of God.*

May you walk all your days grounded in that identity, which is the truest thing about you.

And may you have eyes to see that everyone around you is *also* a loved and fully accepted child of God.

Peace be with you.

AFTERWORD

---------------------->

THEN AND NOW:
A REFLECTION ON
UNCLOBBER

His words stung, piercing my doe-eyed, first-time author enthusiasm. Here was a guy I'd long admired and finally met at an event in Minnesota, opining on my remark about trying to finish the manuscript for my first book, to be titled, *UnClobber: Rethinking Our Misuse of the Bible on Homosexuality.*

"Part of the book will chronicle my journey of shifting away from the evangelicalism of my roots and toward an open and affirming theology," I blathered, trying to quickly convey the book's concept before he lost interest and moved on to the next person in line, "while the other chapters explore the six passages historically used to justify discrimination against those who identify as LGBTQ."

"Hmm," he grunted, nodding his head just enough to feign interest. And that's when he uttered the words that shadowed in doubt the previous six months I had spent on writing. "I kinda think that issue is behind us. I'm not sure people will be interested in that."

"Uh . . . oh . . . okay, well it was nice to meet you. Thanks again for your work in the world." I walked away, deflated. Only two months stood between me and the deadline for *UnClobber*, and now I wondered if I was embarking on a fool's errand.

This guy had been in the industry for a long time and authored multiple books. He'd been influential in some of the earliest movements of the evangelical exodus. For two decades he'd been engaging with this sort of material. And how did he respond upon hearing that my first book would tackle the topic of the Bible and homosexuality? By shrugging it off like it I was Blackberry trying to compete with Apple after the iPhone launched: adorable, but people have moved on.

I believe he intended no disrespect. Unnecessarily blunt? Sure. But meant to crush my spirit and make me wonder if I'd wasted the past year of my life? Doubtful. Yet that was the impact as I lay in my hotel room later that night. *Who's gonna buy this book if he's right?*

Of course, back in 2015 my sense was that people — like myself — were still wrestling with this stuff. I assumed (hoped?) there was still a real need for easy-to-read, accessible resources on the topic.

But what did I know?

Not Obsolete . . . Yet

The fact that you're reading this right now is evidence that my (now) friend from the lobby was dead wrong. In almost every year that it's been out, *UnClobber* has sold more copies than the year before. Interest in this subject, and the need for resources, has only *increased* since its debut. Turns out, the subject of the Bible and homosexuality is far, far from being behind us.

To be sure, American culture has made massive gains in the past few decades. Transport a gay man or a lesbian woman from the '70s to today and they wouldn't believe their eyes. Openly gay politicians in some of the most prominent places of power? Same-sex marriage legalized by the Supreme Court? Almost all Fortune 500 companies now including sexual orientation and gender identity in their antidiscrimination polices? Entire media enterprises created by LGBTQ people? Conversion therapies made illegal and entire organizations committed to "ex-gay" ideology shuttered? *Ellen DeGeneres, Laverne Cox, and Neil Patrick Harris?!*

We've traveled some distances, y'all.

Even in the church world, which is always at least twenty years behind secular culture, we've seen massive gains in the number of queer clergy, resources for LGBTQ youth, and entire denominations shifting toward affirming theology. Across the board, acceptance of homosexuality has risen in every Protestant denomination.[1]

And yet, at the same time, Christian churches, schools, and communities are still some of the least safe places for those who identify LGBTQ. Especially among evangelical churches, traditional theology that maintains homosexuality to be a sin, that denies the sanctity of same-sex marriages, and that does not honor the reality of transgender people retains prominence. But what's also true is that people are shifting away from these more conservative spaces at an alarming rate, in no small part because of the church's continued rejection and oppression of LGBTQ individuals. This has made texts like *UnClobber* increasingly sought after as more and more people experience what I refer to in the opening chapter as a misalignment between the head and the heart.

On one hand, I'm extremely grateful for the success of this book, not because of the success itself, but because of what it means. It means that thousands of people have been liberated from tragic and toxic misunderstandings of the Bible. It means thousands of LGBTQ people have been able to finally see themselves as God sees them: beloved and beautiful. It means thousands of friends and family members have been able to overcome the bad theology that held them back from fully embracing their LGBTQ loved ones. So yeah, it is a very good thing that this book has reached so many people.

And, on the other hand, I can't wait until this book is truly and finally obsolete. I can't wait for the day when nobody opens up Google and types, "Is homosexuality a sin?" I can't wait for the email from my publisher that says, "Due to a lack of sales, we are taking *UnClobber* out of print."

The day will come when the thought of needing to reconcile faith and sexuality seems absurd. The day will come when the idea that the Bible (or God) opposes LGBTQ people will be in our distant memory. But, to quote Aragorn as he rallied the soldiers of Gondor to the final battle at the Black Gate of Mordor, "It is not this day!"

In the meantime, I'm honored and grateful to do this work. What a joy to not only get to publish *UnClobber* at all, but now, six years after its release, here we are releasing a second edition with a study guide and an extra chapter, this here afterword.

As I reflect back on these last few years, I thought I'd share with you some of what I've learned, what I wish I'd done differently, and what I think now about the future.

It's Clunky for Me (a Straight, Cisgender Guy) to Do This Work

Right after *UnClobber* came out, some of the first backlash came not from the sources I anticipated—conservative evangelicals on the right—but from members of the gay community on the left. Some took umbrage with the fact that I, a cisgender, heterosexual man, was writing about anything having to do with homosexuality.

At first, I did what almost all cis-het guys do: I got defensive. I argued. I insisted that "I'm trying to help, here!" I couldn't believe that my work was being criticized by some of the very same people I was trying to be an ally for. Basically, as is evidenced by the first word of the past four sentences, I completely centered myself.

It took me awhile to really hear (and, truth be told, I'm still listening and learning) the very valid criticism from those who are disillusioned that yet another straight pastor guy was writing on this topic. They're not wrong; that is frustrating. We (people with my same identity markers) have taken up most of the oxygen in most of the rooms for a really long time. And even though some of the early pushback was, in my mind, inaccurate (e.g. it assumed *UnClobber* was *about homosexuality* as an orientation and/or experience, rather than about the *Bible* and how it has been misused), the overall point I think still has merit. It is clunky for someone who's not in the marginalized community to do work for/within/on-behalf-of those who are.

I've also learned that there's not a universal opinion on this topic. Some marginalized people believe that allyship itself is problematic. Others believe that the only role allies should play is to shut up and sit down, to pass the mic, and to permit (in this case) only LGBTQ people to speak out. Others believe that it will take all of us doing our part, in our own ways, to move matters of injustice *toward* justice. While it can be tricky to do so, I'm learning to hold space for all the perspectives and all the feelings, because they all belong.

So yes, I get it: it's frustrating that someone like me wrote this book and has potentially taken opportunities away from LGBTQ authors and speakers to have their voices heard. The complications of such an arrangement are real, and the pushback is understandable.

One of the things I've tried to be intentional about over the past several years is to use whatever influence or platform I have to elevate the voices of LGBTQ people, to highlight their work, and to point people toward it. My thoughts on this topic are not the best thoughts, nor should they be the only ones we engage with. This is something I've been learning and trying to improve on. I wish I had better awareness of this years ago so that I could have named this tension in the first edition of *UnClobber* (and then not gotten so defensive when the criticism came). While it wouldn't have mattered to everyone (because again, some people—and for reasons I totally respect—feel people like me shouldn't write books like this at all), I do believe that naming this and honoring it is the right thing to do.

At the same time, I'll continue doing my best to keep going with this important work because another thing I've learned is that, for some people, the fact that I *am* straight actually makes a book like *UnClobber* all the more impactful and effective. "I've read some of the other books in this field," they tell me often, "but it wasn't until reading *your* book that the pieces finally fell into place."

To be sure, this is not because *UnClobber* is academically superior to other books like it. It is not. Nor is it because I'm a better writer. Rather, I think this has been true for so many people because—and this is especially the case from the LGBTQ readers who have reached out to me—when they read another book by an author who's gay, it's as though there's this nagging little voice in the back of their mind the whole time that whispers, "Well sure, of course, the author says that, because they're gay and they're needing to justify their orientation." Whereas, because I didn't have a horse in the race—neither for myself nor, as mentioned in chapter 7, even a close friend or family member—when they read my words, the ideas and arguments appear to be more neutral. As a result, my perspective has allowed many readers to not just *hear* that the Bible truly does not condemn them but begin to *believe* it for the first time as well.

However, I've thought a lot about it over the years, and I think there's another reason for this phenomenon. I think there is a kind of healing from trauma that takes place when we reencounter some of the factors of the thing that first wounded us, but in a wildly different context where there is safety, trust, and no judgment. This is part of why talk therapy works, because we revisit some of the painful emotional places from our past, in our therapist's office, where our stories, experiences, and feelings are met with care, compassion, and no judgment. As a result, our brain can begin the work of rewiring itself by connecting new emotional experiences ("I am safe, I am loved, I am okay") to those old memories.

Most people who've ever been told by a church or a religious community that they are destined for hell because they are gay have been told that by a cis-het male pastor. And even if such messages came from home or from a female voice, there is still a strong probability that the original source behind those messages were—you guessed it—from the teachings and writings of cis-het Christian men.

So when someone like me, who is both *like* the youth pastor from back home and also very much *unlike* him, the brain gets an opportunity to begin making new connections, replacing the voice of preachers in their past who took up residency in their hearts and minds, convincing them they were an abomination. Hearing—or in this case, reading— the words of an affirming preacher provides new and better voices to move them toward the truth of their belovedness.

Not Just Sons and Daughters

One of the things I'm sad about with regard to how I originally wrote *UnClobber* was my failure to use gender inclusive language. Sadly, I hadn't met Alex yet back when I wrote the first edition.

On an otherwise uneventful Sunday afternoon several years ago, while the band packed up their gear and the cleanup crew stacked chairs, my new friend Alex approached me wanting to talk. We scooted off to the side of the elementary cafeteria for a bit more privacy. His eyes looked anxious yet kind.

"Pastor Colby," he began, and I noted the use of *pastor*, a formality rarely used around Sojourn. "Every Sunday you talk about the love of God, and how we are all loved by God, and I want you to know I am here for that. Such positive messages are part of why I come every week. But can I offer you a bit of feedback on some of the ways you talk about it?"

Alex and I had spoken before, and I trusted his experience and insight. "Yes, please, by all means."

"Well, you always use the phrase 'loved sons and daughters of God,' which is a lovely sentiment, but as an intersex, transgender man, I don't necessarily hear myself in those two terms. I'm not sure I'm a son of God, and I know I'm not a daughter of God. So I wonder if you'd consider using something broader and more inclusive, such as *children of God*?"

My eyes widened. "Oh my goodness, Alex, yes, of course! You are absolutely right. That makes so much sense. I'm sorry I hadn't been doing that already, and I commit to changing how I talk about our identities as the beloved of God."

Fortunately, I had an Alex in my life to bring awareness to the ways in which the language we use can serve to further entrench binaries that reinforce exclusionary postures. At least fourteen times in the original edition of *UnClobber*, I wrote a version of the phrase "LGBTQ brothers and sisters," with a couple mentions about being a beloved "son or daughter" of God. Knowing what I know now about things such as intersex and gender identity, I see how such language excludes. I hadn't yet learned this prior to Alex teaching me, and ever since that day, I've tried to change how I talk and write.

Therefore, in this second edition of *UnClobber*, you'll notice that all references to LGBTQ brothers and sisters or sons and daughters has been changed to *siblings* or *children*. To anyone who read the original version and, like Alex, felt unseen or erased, I apologize. I hope this newer version represents you and honors you better.

Speaking of honoring you better, I'd also like to acknowledge that throughout the book I used the term *LGBTQ* when, in reality, the scope of *UnClobber* deals primarily with the Bible and homosexuality—not so much topics related to transgender people. Trans people and their experience get erased enough as it is in our culture, and I understand how using the term *LGBTQ* as essentially synonymous with "gay and lesbian" furthers that erasure. To be clear, the Bible has similarly been misused to justify discrimination against those who are transgender, and by no means did I intend to suggest otherwise by limiting the scope of *UnClobber* to homosexuality. For a fuller treatment of this topic, I recommend you read *Transforming: The Bible and the Lives of Transgender Christians* by Austen Hartke, who demonstrates how trans people have similarly been Clobbered by cherry-picked, poorly translated passages.

It's Not the Spirit, It's Your Brain

Next, I'd like to take a moment to address one of the most frequent questions I've been asked since *UnClobber* released. It goes something like this: "Colby, I want to believe what you're saying, that the Bible doesn't actually condemn me, but I still feel icky when I hold my partner's hand. I still feel guilty when I think about marrying them someday. What if that's the Holy Spirit convicting me?" I've been surprised at how often this comes up, so let me offer a brief response here for future readers.

First, you're totally normal and this makes so much sense. You've spent years, maybe even decades, living out one particular narrative: homosexuality is a sin, and you cannot be both gay and Christian. Life is rarely simple, and there isn't a switch you can flip to wake up one day with all new ideas and their accompanying feelings.

Plus, I think sometimes we can get confused between what might be the Spirit of God prompting us in our hearts and what might be just the residue of ideas deep in our brain being dislodged. Consider how, for many people, we grew up hearing religious ideas taught directly alongside standard education about the world. Which means that about the same time you were learning 2+2=4 and how photosynthesis works, you also might've been told ideas about who God is, what the Bible is, and how you're a depraved human who is very much unworthy of being in God's presence. Your sweet little brain did not have one bucket for "things that are mathematically and scientifically true, therefore lock these down," and another for "things that are religiously true, therefore hold these loosely so that you can possibly adapt later in life." No, you just dumped everything you learned in one large bucket of "things that are true."

Fast forward to today, and imagine you just read an entire book inviting you to consider that 2+2 does not actually equal 4. We would expect you to have resistance. We would anticipate strain as you tried to unlearn old ideas and reimagine new ones. So when someone suggests to you that what you've always been told about the Bible might not be true or that the ideas you used to have in your head about who God is might benefit from being updated, your brain understandably might be less than enthused to entertain such notions.

My point is, next time you're tempted to think that maybe the feeling of discomfort in your belly is the Holy Spirit convicting you of sin, and so maybe you should try harder to be straight just *one more time*, may you instead honor that this is your brain doing the hard work of unlearning. And of course, it will take time for your body to adjust and settle into these new data points now setting up shop in your "things that are true" brain bucket.

People Can and Do Change

Somewhere along the way I picked up the widely believed assumption that people don't change. After doing this *UnClobber* work for a decade, I can safely say that's rubbish.

I recently got a message from a guy I'd corresponded with eighteen months ago when he reached out with questions. Like many who contact me, he was struggling to find a pathway toward fully loving and accepting his gay child. I hadn't heard from him since our initial interaction, during which I challenged several of his preconceived ideas rooted in rather antiquated views of sex and sexuality. Rereading his initial message was shocking because of the degree to which he was immersed in ignorance and fear. However, over the past year and a half, he's done a lot of soul searching and asking God to help him see with new eyes. His most recent message included a celebration of a new understanding of the vastness of love, opening up all new channels for him to fully accept and embrace his child—which included walking her down the aisle at her wedding! Incredible.

And that's just the tip of the iceberg of the stories I've heard over these past six years, as I've been given the gift of a front-row seat to people's lives. Over and over again, folks are able to put behind them the bad theology of their conservative roots and become entirely transformed by the renewing of their mind, figuring out along the way the good and pleasing will of God (Rom. 12:2, anyone?).

I've seen men set free from the chains of deadly theology, finally liberated to be who they are and find love with another man. I've seen women empowered to leave behind the narrow-mindedness of their family systems so that they could love who they are enough to love and be loved by another woman. I've seen mothers rejoice at discovering the Bible does not, in fact, reduce their child to a wicked, depraved abomination. I've seen fathers' relationships with their children restored after years of fracturing because Dad wasn't able to accept their child as trans—story after story of people literally changing their minds about the Bible and LGBTQ identities and, as a result, changing their lives and the lives of people around them.

And yet, I've also seen the heartache of those whose loved ones haven't yet changed. I know that many of you have sent a copy of *UnClobber* to your mom, hoping she'd read it. I've heard from those of you who prayed that your dad might finally accept you for who you are, yet you still haven't heard from him in years. The pain of waiting to be loved is a pain all unto itself. Hope can hurt, which is why many people seal off that cavern of their heart. They convince themselves it is best to just move on, to stop waiting for grandpa to come around because he never will. You know what, you might be right. Maybe he never will.

But can I tell you a secret?... *You also might be wrong.* Who can ever know how, when, or why people change when they do? Isn't that just grace, a gift that appears to come from nowhere? Think about your own life and some of the significant changes you've experienced. Could you ever have seen those coming?

That's why I'd like to close this little addition to this second edition with a word of empathy and an invitation to hope.

To you who are still waiting to be invited home for Christmas, I'm sorry.

To you who are still waiting for your romantic partner to be invited as well and to be treated like part of the family, I'm sorry.

To you who are still waiting to feel not just welcome in your home but fully celebrated, I'm sorry.

To you who are still waiting for your grandparents, your siblings, your cousins to stop treating you like you're the enemy and to love you as you are, I'm sorry.

To you who are still waiting for the day when you'll fully be able to love and accept yourself, untethered from the years of harmful teaching you were given, I'm sorry.

To you who are lonely because this world is unkind and in so, so many ways we are not a friendly place for those outside what society has considered "normal," I'm sorry.

To you who've already lost people you love who are no longer alive or able to come around on this particular topic, I'm sorry.

I pray that the same God who mysteriously swept me along in my journey toward full inclusion of LGBTQ people will so move in the hearts and minds of your loved ones as well.

I pray that the same God who transformed Saul of Tarsus—persecutor of Christians—into the apostle Paul—evangelist for the gospel—might transform that one person in your life who you never thought would come around.

I pray that hope—vulnerable and scary though it may be—will fill every corner of your soul, daring you to never close off your heart.

I pray you shower yourself in kindness and compassion because life is hard. May you treat yourself at least as well as a loving, compassionate God would want you to be treated.

I pray the years of hard work you've put into showing the non-affirming people in your life that you can, in fact, be gay *and* live a flourishing life will one day show them just how full of God's light and love you are.

Looking back at the past six years since this book came out, I can honestly say I never could have imagined just how drastically my view of humanity's capacity to change would alter.

Friends, I know we're supposed to look at the resurrection of Jesus as being this unprecedented, singular event that proved his divinity and affirms the truth of

Christianity. It happened to him and no one else, a one-time stroke of the Divine.

But the more I do this work, the more I think, "Yes, but also, I see people coming back from the dead
all
the
time."

May it be so for you, for your loved ones, and for all who are still asleep in their misunderstandings of the Bible.
Amen.

ACKNOWLEDGMENTS

——————————————————→

I remember the first time I walked through a BevMo and gawked at their outrageous beer selection. So many options. So many *good* options. But my wallet (and my liver) mandated moderation. In order to walk out successfully, some IPAs and stouts didn't make it in the shopping cart.

For my first published book, writing the Acknowledgments feels similar. The number of people I could thank and acknowledge, who have played a role in my life and who helped *UnClobber* get to this point, are more than can fit here. But to leave empty-handed would be a shame.

Therefore, because I was the recipient of such gratuitous inspiration, affirmation, and encouragement, I would like to thank the following individuals without whom *UnClobber* might forever remain an unfinished blog series that literally tens of people might have read.

My editor at Westminster John Knox Press, Jessica Miller Kelley, who took a chance on me after hearing me talk for precisely seven minutes about Legos, homosexuality, and getting fired.

The staff (Jessica, Mathew, Jessica, Sarah, Eric) and elders (Larry, Vicky, Michelle, Daniel, Mary Jo, Dane, Merrilee, Carrie) at Sojourn who have never stopped believing that I am enough. They remind me every week that I'm the most blessed man to do what I do with all of you. You make leading a church fun . . . as it should be.

The following shapers of thought have forever altered my mind and heart, and I thank you for your work and your selves, and how you have impacted my life both personally and professionally: Glennon Doyle Melton, Rob Bell, Brian McLaren, Richard Beck, Doug Pagitt, and Kristen Howerton.

The particularly fabulous friends and family who stood by Kate and me during the hard days and helped us find our way again: Logan, Kyle, Justin, Meghan, Irma, Laura, James, Nic, Tara, and others too numerous to include.

To the Sojourn Grace Collective family, a hearty dose of light and love for all of you. You have given me hope that the Way of Jesus is still worth chasing. And you put up with some so-so sermons for a stretch of time while I finished writing this book. *GONG* *I did it! I wrote my first book!* *THUNDEROUS APPLAUSE*

You providers of time and space, who gave of your resources so that I might find time to focus on writing *UnClobber*: Larry, Cory, Elisa, Vicky, Chas, and Autumn. And also, the creator of the "Deep Focus" playlist on Spotify. Your background jams for writing are on point.

To my four sons, I thank you for reflecting to me joy, humility, grace, and love. Zeke, Tai, Jae, and Huck, you are amazing people, I am so proud of you, and so grateful you gave Daddy time away from you to work on writing his first book. I realize it is not as awesome as Shel Silverstein, *Diary of a Wimpy Kid*, Percy Jackson, or *The Book with No Pictures*, but I'd still love to read this to you every night before bed. (I'm kidding . . . we'll take Thursday nights off.)

And finally, Kate, thank you most of all. For reasons unbeknownst to me, you have never doubted that I could do this. I drew on your strength so many times it's amazing you can still walk. Not only did you provide every ounce of support and encouragement I needed to write this book, but you also contributed so much to the content, the shape, and most especially the voicing. Thank you for reminding me of who I am, who we are. You gave and gave and gave to ensure that *UnClobber* came to life, so anyone who reads this book owes you gratitude. (Assuming they like the book. If they don't, then I guess they can blame me.)

SMALL GROUP STUDY GUIDE

───────────────────►

Reassessing long-held beliefs about the Bible can be not just an intellectual challenge but an emotional one too. When those beliefs concern not just your commitment to Scripture but the very lives and dignity of other people — maybe even yourself—the stakes are especially high. To wrestle with these things in community with other people of faith who come from a different starting point, have walked different roads, and carry different baggage takes courage and compassion.

This study guide covers two chapters per session so that you can study *UnClobber* in six sessions, reading approximately thirty pages in preparation for each discussion. Session 6 includes less reading to allow time for more conversation and processing at the completion of the study. As the book alternates between chapters telling the author's personal story as a pastor shifting away from previously held beliefs about the Bible and LGBTQ affirmation and chapters examining the Scriptures that are often used to condemn homosexuality, each session explores both personal beliefs and experiences, and biblical study.

Session 1: Using and Misusing the Bible—introduction, prologue, and chapters 1 and 2

Session 2: Sin, Sex, and Sodom—chapters 3 and 4

Session 3: The Bonds and Boundaries of Community—
  chapters 5 and 6

Session 4: Jews, Gentiles, and Judgment—chapters 7
  and 8

Session 5: Healthy and Unhealthy Sex—chapters 9 and
  10

Session 6: Where Do We Go from Here?—afterword

Each session begins with a brief affirmation to be read aloud. Depending on the preferences and context of your group, consider allowing a period of silence for personal meditation and/or a brief prayer.

Knowing that some people are slower to speak than others, be intentional about inviting each person to respond to each question and allowing them to pass if they do not wish to speak at that time. Recognize that everyone comes to the group with different ideas, backgrounds, and perspectives. Do your best to foster an environment in which everyone feels heard and valued. Pay particular attention to members of your group who are part of the LGBTQ community, recognizing how discussion of the Clobber Passages may bring up painful feelings and past experiences of having these texts used against them. Assure all group members that they are welcome to step out of the room at any time to attend to their mental health.

SESSION 1: USING AND MISUSING THE BIBLE

Readings: introduction, prologue, and chapters 1 and 2
Focus Scripture: 2 Timothy 3:14–17

Opening Affirmation
God is big enough for our questions. God is the answer.
God is love.

Questions for Discussion
1. When did you first become aware of LGBTQ identities? Do you have a memory of meeting someone, seeing something on TV, or having a conversation about
   homosexuality?
2. When did you first become aware of condemnation
   against LGBTQ people? Did you receive specific messages from parents or church leaders?
3. Have you ever experienced your head and heart being
   out of alignment, as the author describes? How did you
   resolve that tension—or have you?
4. Have you ever said or done anything similar to the
   author's impromptu apology to the gay couple on the
   train (pp. 16–17)? What happened?
5. Have you ever (intentionally or unintentionally) misused the Bible like the author describes on pages
   19–21? When did you realize that your interpretation
   or reasoning was flawed?
6. Were you aware of or familiar with the Clobber Passages before beginning this book? If so, how did they
   influence your thinking about sexual ethics?
7. What is the Bible's role in your faith? How would
   you complete the following sentence? *The Bible
   is* _____.
8. Read 2 Timothy 3:14-17. What does this passage mean
   to you? Have you ever felt "Clobbered" by this passage
   of Scripture?

SESSION 2: SIN, SEX, AND SODOM
Readings: chapters 3 and 4
Focus Scripture: Genesis 19:1–11

Opening Affirmation
There is room for everyone.

Questions for Discussion
1. What do you think of the concept the author calls "The Naaman Effect" (pp. 34–35), stating that it's okay if your actions do not fully reflect your convictions—especially if those convictions are new? How long do you think this effect can last before the feeling of hypocrisy becomes too strong?
2. Do you agree that "there is no room for discrimination in the Kingdom of God" (p. 36)? Do you ever find yourself making exceptions to that idea?
3. How do you feel about expressing your convictions publicly, whether verbally or on social media? Do you tend to fear others' reactions to your statements?
4. Reflecting on the mantra of "in essentials, unity; in non-essentials, liberty; in all things, charity," do you think doctrines around sexuality are essential? What about our definition of sin?
5. Could you retell the story of Sodom and Gomorrah from memory before reading chapter 4? What would you have identified as "the sin of Sodom"?
6. Read Genesis 19:1–11. Why do we imagine this mob (including every man of the town) as a group of lust-ful gay men rather than violent xenophobic men? How does this relate to our view of rape?
7. Read Ezekiel 16:49–50. How did God's people who heard the tale of Sodom and Gomorrah within centuries of its origin interpret the moral of the story?

8. Why do we so readily identify sin as sexual in nature while ignoring sins like pride, selfishness, and refusal to help those in need? How could we change that?

SESSION 3: THE BONDS AND BOUNDARIES OF COMMUNITY

Readings: chapters 5 and 6
Focus Scripture: Leviticus 18:22 and 20:13

Opening Affirmation
In all things, love.

Questions for Discussion
1. Have arguments over homosexuality been a point of contention in your faith community or one you've previously been part of? Why do you think this one issue has such power to divide churches?
2. Do you agree with the author's statement to the church board on page 70, that it is possible "to think that homosexuality is a sin but also believe that discrimination against the gay community . . . is not okay"? Have you ever held a both-and position like this on any issue?
3. Do you think it is important for a church—or even just its pastors—to be united in their convictions on full inclusion of the LGBTQ community? How does such unity or diversity of belief affect LGBTQ people within the congregation?
4. Some Christians say that the Old Testament Law does not apply anymore. Some make a distinction between various laws being culturally bound and some expressing universal moral rules. What meaning does the Old Testament Law have for you?
5. Read Leviticus 18:22 and 20:13. In light of the background the author provides on pages 82–85, what significance do you think these passages would have had for the Hebrew community receiving the Law?
6. How does the ambiguity of translation affect the way you read these passages? Does the modifying phrase "as with a woman" suggest there is an acceptable way for males to lie with males?

7. How is the meaning of *abomination* different from how we typically use the word? Can you think of things today that are not sinful but "transgress a cultural boundary"?

8. What would you say to the man on page 95 wondering how he, as a gay man, would have been received in the ancient Hebrew community?

SESSION 4: JEWS, GENTILES, AND JUDGEMENT

Readings: chapters 7 and 8
Focus Scripture: Romans 1:26–27

Opening Affirmation
Difference is an invitation. Diversity leads to understanding.

Questions for Discussion
1. What kind of church do you long for? What kind of church do you think our LGBTQ siblings long for?
2. How diverse is your church? What are the strengths and challenges of diversity in a faith community?
3. On pages 104–6, the author discusses how many people rethink their position on homosexuality when they learn a loved one is gay. Do you think that personal relationships make reevaluated beliefs more or less genuine?
4. Read Romans 1:26–27. Do you agree with the author and "Josh" (pp. 114–15) that this is the most challenging of the Clobber Passages to UnClobber?
5. According to the author, why did Paul include the "self-contained discourse" accusing Gentiles of all sorts of depravity?
6. Read Romans 2:1–3. Even without the knowledge of Paul's rhetorical device, does this change your reading of the paragraphs that precede it?
7. How might this Clobber Passage—in the context of how Paul "springs the trap" on his Jewish readers (see pp. 123–27)—be a lesson to the church today for dealing with diversity, prejudice, and the perceived sins of others?
8. Given the distinct culture into which Paul was writing, with its taboos against non-procreative sex even among heterosexuals and its practices of pederasty and sexual rituals in pagan temples, how should biblical sexual ethics be applied by Christians today?

SESSION 5: HEALTHY AND UNHEALTHY SEX
Readings: chapters 9 and 10
Focus Scripture: 1 Corinthians 6:9 and 1 Timothy 1:10

Opening Affirmation
Sex takes many forms. Some honor God, ourselves, and one another. Some do not.

Questions for Discussion
1. What messages were you taught as a child that you later had to be deprogrammed from? What would have been more helpful to be told as you grew up?
2. If you could start a church from scratch, what would it be like? Does the type of gathering described on pages 144–47 appeal to you? Why or why not?
3. Have you ever received messages in a church context that have helped you "lay groundwork for creating healthy sexual boundaries" or be "committed to loving ourselves and our neighbor *even when it comes to our sexual activities*" (p. 151)? What would such a sexual ethic look like?
4. What happens when you flip the script, as the author does on page 153, and ask "Is heterosexuality a sin?"
5. Read 1 Corinthians 6:9 and 1 Timothy 1:10. What words does your translation use? Compare several translations. What are the implications of those word choices for modern readers?
6. How do the nuances of the words *malakoi* and *arsenokoitai* suggest that these Clobber Passages are specifically about sexual exploitation?
7. How does it affect your thinking to know that *natural eunuchs*—men who were simply not aroused by or inclined to procreate with women—were acknowledged by Jesus and his contemporaries? What does that knowledge mean in light of the Clobber Passages?

8. On page 170, the author lays out several types of readers and how they might have approached this book. Which sounds most like you? Did the author accomplish with you what he had hoped?

SESSION 6: WHERE DO WE GO FROM HERE?

Reading: afterword
Focus Scripture: Deuteronomy 23:1 and Isaiah 56:4–5

Opening Affirmation
The Lord gathers the outcasts.

Questions for Discussion
1. Have you ever thought that the question of LGBTQ inclusion was settled or that everyone whose mind could ever be changed had already been changed?
2. What do you think the role of allies should be, whether in the fight for LGBTQ equality, racial justice, or gender equality? Where is the line between standing up for the marginalized and taking opportunities away from those in the marginalized community?
3. The "T" in LGBTQ is often overlooked and is not addressed in this book on the Bible and homosexuality. There are different Bible passages used to Clobber trans and other gender-nonconforming people. Using the analytical skills you have learned in previous sessions, how might these two passages often used against trans persons be UnClobbered? (Hints are offered in parentheses to prompt your thinking.)

   — Genesis 1:27 (Compare with the other binaries of creation named, e.g. day and night, land and water.)
   — Deuteronomy 22:5 (Does this remind you of the Leviticus passages discussed in session 3?)

4. Read Deuteronomy 23:1, which excludes from the assembly men whose genitals have been altered (whether by accident or intentionally, it would seem). Then read Isaiah 56:4–5. What do you make of this reversal/negation of the earlier prohibition?

5. Imagine being a eunuch in ancient Israel hearing Isaiah declare the prophecy written down in Isaiah 56. Would you have had trouble believing those words of blessing were really from God? How do you know when a nagging feeling is from the Holy Spirit and when it is just the "residue of ideas deep in our brain being dislodged," as the author says on page 186?
6. Who have you known who—despite being adamant and inflexible in their conviction—has opened their mind and changed perspective on an issue of moral importance? How did that change come about?
7. Who are you hoping will experience such a change in perspective? Who might be hoping the same for you, and why? How do you feel about that?
8. What next steps will you take to ensure that no one feels Clobbered by Scripture?

SERMON SERIES GUIDE

⟶

This outline for a six-week sermon series corresponds with the themes of the *UnClobber* study guide such that your congregation can deeply engage with the Scriptures, sexual ethics, and LGBTQ inclusion both in their small group discussions and during worship. This series can serve as a profound part of your congregation's process of becoming an open and affirming church and as a way of equipping allies to defend LGBTQ inclusion with non-affirming Christians.

In addition to small group study offerings, you may also choose to offer affinity group gatherings for LGBTQ persons, parents of LGBTQ kids, etc., to provide support, connection, and the opportunity to debrief these messages together.

In addition to the exegesis in this book, you will likely want to consult additional commentaries and various translations of the Bible as you prepare to preach on the Clobber Passages. The sermon starters below offer suggestions for approaching each message as well as a main takeaway to focus your planning around. For additional inspiration, see Colby Martin's online video courses and free printable cheat sheets on each Clobber Passage at www.unclobber.com.

SERMON 1: USING AND MISUSING THE BIBLE

Focus Scripture: 2 Timothy 3:14–17

Main Takeaway: The Bible is a source of wisdom and should not be used as a weapon.

This opening sermon in the series introduces the church's legacy of doing harm to the LGBTQ community and the problem of using the Bible to Clobber, well, anyone. Share your own history with biblical interpretation overall—especially if you've ever been guilty of misusing the Bible—and with regard to the Clobber Passages specifically. Explore what the oft-quoted 2 Timothy 3:16 passage means to you and how it can become a Clobber Passage in itself for those trying to defend a literalist or *sola Scriptura* approach to the Bible. Starting at verse 14, you can confront people's fears and anxieties about questioning things they've heard and believed since childhood—honoring the journey of continued growth and learning—as you articulate a loving, Christ-centered hermeneutic for your congregation.

SERMON 2: SIN, SEX, AND SODOM

Focus Scripture: Genesis 19:1–11

Main Takeaway: The "sin of Sodom" has nothing to do with sex.

The tale of Sodom and Gomorrah has attained mythic status in the Judeo-Christian tradition, even as many people are fuzzy on the details. As you tackle this first of the Clobber Passages, consider offering a couple trigger warnings, for gay men in particular, as the word *Sodomite* has been especially dehumanizing, and also for those impacted by rape—as you'll likely use the word (or something similar to it), which can be very unsettling for some. You may want to introduce the story of Baucis and Philemon (see p. 50) or start with the story of Abraham's hospitality in Genesis 18 to emphasize the importance of hospitality in ancient culture and contrast the men of Sodom's xenophobic rage with Lot's effusive welcome. Central to UnClobbering this passage is the distinction between gang rape and gay sex—or rape and sex, period—as we clarify Sodom's true sin as recalled in Ezekiel 16:49–50.

SERMON 3: THE BONDS AND BOUNDARIES OF COMMUNITY
Focus Scriptures: Leviticus 18:22 and 20:13

Main Takeaway: Levitical Law was created for a specific people and purpose.

You might begin this message by exploring different types of rules: there are criminal laws with infractions punishable with fines and imprisonment; there are house rules to keep family life safe and orderly; there are unspoken rules about what's not appropriate in certain settings and might earn you some funny looks. There are many assumptions and beliefs about the Old Testament Law and what it means for Christians today, but it is central to examine what the Law meant for the Hebrew people just establishing their community and identity as a people. The Holiness Code had a clear purpose in promoting group distinctiveness and preserving familial bonds. Emphasize the original meaning of *abomination* and the ambiguity of *mishkevey ishsha* to show that Leviticus does not condemn same-sex relationships as we know them today.

SERMON 4: JEWS, GENTILES, AND JUDGEMENT

Focus Scripture: Romans 1:26–27

Main Takeaway: Judging others is more sinful than any sexual act.

The context of the church at Rome, with deep divisions between Jewish and Gentile Christians, offers an opportunity to address discord within our churches today. The UnClobbering of this passage has three main points: (1) Paul was likely utilizing a rhetorical device, citing the prejudicial discourses some Jews were using against Gentiles at the time, to call attention to their conflict. (2) Even if Paul happened to agree with those characterizations of Gentiles' wickedness, the sexual acts described include non-procreative heterosexual sex, public lewdness, and pagan rituals, not same-sex relationships as we know them today. (3) Paul springs a trap in Romans 2, scolding all those who would judge others and reminding them that God is the only righteous judge. Right there with this Clobber Passage is Paul's clear admonition not to Clobber one another with judgment but to attend to our own sins and trust God with the rest.

SERMON 5: HEALTHY AND UNHEALTHY SEX

Focus Scriptures: 1 Corinthians 6:9 and 1 Timothy 1:10

Main Takeaway: Whatever your orientation, sex should not be exploitative.

These final Clobber Passages are the only two to use the word *homosexuality*—but only in certain English translations and only in the last seventy-five years—presenting an opportunity to share some of the history around that word choice. The Greek words Paul uses in these verses are somewhat ambiguous, but using the context of the surrounding chapters in 1 Corinthians 5–7 and the other vices condemned along with *malakoi* and *arsenokoitai*, it is reasonable to conclude that these sex-related concepts were exploitative in some way. Much as Leviticus laid out the rules of the burgeoning Hebrew community, Paul is laying out the ethical code for what it means to live in the way of Jesus. While this code also includes certain sexual behaviors, the reasoning is not based in sexual orientation (a foreign concept at the time) but in how we treat one another in the Christian community.

SERMON 6: WHERE DO WE GO FROM HERE?

Focus Scripture: Deuteronomy 23:1 and Isaiah 56:4–5

Main Takeaway: There is still work to be done to UnClobber all of God's children.

This sermon aims to sum up the series with an overall message of affirmation and an invitation to look toward next steps. Will your church go public as LGBTQ affirming? Will you open your space to same-gender weddings and designate an all-gender bathroom? Consider what other people are being Clobbered by Scripture, starting with the *T* in LGBTQ. Deuteronomy 23:1 (as well as Deut. 22:5 and Gen. 1:27) have been used to condemn and exclude transgender people and everyone who falls outside the gender binary. However, Scripture itself offers not only a message of inclusion but an example of evolving thought and growing openness. Isaiah 56:4–5 specifically overrides the policy of exclusion stated in Deuteronomy 23, and in the surrounding verses (Isa. 56:3–8) issues a resounding welcome to not just the gender diverse but "foreigners" and other "outcasts" as well. Our churches are called to share this radical message of welcome in order to truly be "a house of prayer for all peoples" (v. 7b).

NOTES

Chapter 1: When the Head and the Heart Can't Get Along

1. A "Jesus Juke," aptly named by Jon Acuff on his website Stuff Christians Like, is when you take any conversation and swiftly and abruptly turn it to be about Jesus, with zero regard about whether the Good Lord belonged in the conversation or not.

2. The "Romans Road" is a way of cherry-picking a few verses out of Romans to walk someone along the path of realizing their own sinfulness, confronting their destiny of death and damnation, but becoming privy to how God can save them if they say the right prayer.

3. Thanks to comedian Michael Jr. for introducing me to this wonderfully apropos phrase.

4. "Brutiful" is how Glennon Doyle describes life; as being both brutal *and* beautiful.

5. This word *concern* has become Christianese for, "I'm about to judge you, but I don't want you to be mad at me." Prepare to duck when someone wants to share their "concerns" with you.

6. For more on this, check out Alexander J. Shaia's work at www .quadratos.com.

7. *Thelma & Louise*, directed by Ridley Scott (Beverly Hills, CA: Metro Goldwyn Mayer, 1991), DVD.

Chapter 2: Rethinking Our Misuse of the Bible

1. Second Corinthians 6:14 (ESV); and I sure hope she didn't bother to look up how that verse ends, "for what fellowship has light with darkness?" Ouch. Sorry, Jenny.

2. For the uninitiated, this is *Evangelicalese* for "returned to a sin that I had previously given up for Jesus."

3. Who knows where the legendary *Room 108* would have gone had it not been for that night.

4. "Facts about Suicide," The Trevor Project, https://www.thetrevorproject.org/resources/article/facts-about-lgbtq-youth-suicide.

5. Preeminent Liberation Theologian Gustavo Gutiérrez insists that not only do we read the Bible but also "the Bible reads us and speaks to us." Gustavo Gutiérrez, *On Job: God-Talk and the Suffering of the Innocent* (Maryknoll, NY: Orbis Books, 1987), xvii.

6. Elizabeth Gilbert, *The Signature of All Things* (New York: Viking, 2013), 99. Emphasis in the original.

Chapter 3: How Facebook Got Me Fired

1. His response when asked by a reporter if he thought the Wall should be dismantled.

2. My thanks to Rob Bell for first introducing me to this observation about the story of Naaman.

3. I believe 2011 was also the last year anyone ever went to Yahoo on purpose.

4. I wanted to add *hatred*, but I think that would be lazy on my part. Rarely do Christians "hate" LGBTQ people. It is all about fear, with a dash of ignorance.

5. Earliest source, Marco Antonio de Dominis (1617), "book 4, chapter 8," *De republica ecclesiastica libri X* 1 (London, 1617), 676.

Chapter 4: Reframing the Story of Sodom

1. Martti Nissinen, *Homoeroticism in the Biblical World: A Historical Perspective* (Minneapolis: Fortress Press, 1998), 48.

2. The storyteller mentions Gomorrah before and after the encounter with Lot and the messengers. It was equally destroyed and forever linked with Sodom. So even though we don't read specifically

about the wickedness of Gomorrah, we would be safe in assuming that it was just as wicked.

3. Most recently this is seen in Preston Sprinkle's book, *People to Be Loved* (Zondervan, 2015), which argues the conservative position for all Clobber Passages except this one. "But does Genesis 19 condemn loving, consensual, monogamous gay sex? No, I don't think it does" (p. 43).

Chapter 5: Unfit to Be a Pastor

1. The social gospel began as a movement in the early twentieth century within Protestant America as an effort to re-aim the church's focus on the poor and the outcast. Conservative Christians would later use the term as a shibboleth to root out and reject liberal and mainline Christians because they believed that focusing on the social aspect of a person's life would lead to neglect of his or her spiritual condition.

Chapter 6: Redefining the Boundaries

1. Andrew Peterson, "Come, Lord Jesus," *Carried Along*, Provident Label Group, LLC, 2000.

2. I say "so-called" because the minute you hold up a sign that announces God hates *anyone* is the moment I no longer have to take you seriously as a Christian.

3. This raises the question: If you still believe that people *choose* to be gay, who in their right mind would choose to be something that others call subhuman, vile, and gross?

4. Richard Beck, *Unclean: Meditations on Purity, Hospitality, and Mortality* (Cambridge, England: The Lutterworth Press, 2012), 102.

5. *Horribly* covers a broad spectrum. Yes, holding a "God Hates Fags" placard is unarguably worse than, say, denying a gay person membership in a local church. Yet from the perspective of the oppressed, any oppression is oppression, regardless of degree.

6. This is one of the Thirteen Hermeneutical Rules of Rabbi Ishmael. See Lawrence H. Schiffman, *Texts and Traditions: A Source Reader for the Study of Second Temple and Rabbinic Judaism* (Hoboken, NJ: KTAV Publishing House, Inc., 1998), 532.

7. K. Renato Lings, *Love Lost in Translation* (Bloomington, IN: Trafford, 2013), 203.

8. And don't think it's because it was just *assumed* in the prohibition against male-male sex acts. Leviticus does not shy away from speaking directly to and about women and their conduct with regard to holiness.

9. See also 2 Kgs. 16:3; 21:2; 23:13; 2 Chr. 28:3; 33:2.

10. Jacob Milgrom, *Leviticus* (Minneapolis: Augsburg Fortress, 2004), 196.

Chapter 7: In Search of the Unicorn

1. Not an actual tip for finding unicorns.

2. As I said earlier, though, I recognize that situations like this get messy. Feelings get hurt. Each side thinks the other side is being malicious or vindictive. Accusations about *how* things are said or *when* they're said get lobbied about, as though a "right way" exists to handle ordeals of this nature. So while I'm trying to paint an accurate picture of how my story unfolded and how it felt at the time, I look back now with extra grace for all parties involved, and I realize none of it was personal.

3. I'm sure if he had titled it, "A Pastor Supported the Repeal of DADT, and You'll Never Believe What Happened Next!" then it would have gone viral for sure. But this was 2011; clickbait hadn't been invented yet.

4. I use this phrase provocatively. I don't think it's possible to "deny access to the grace of God." It is freely given, freely flowing, and freely received for all.

5. Curious about my "Depression Beard"? Check out https://vimeo .com/35283967.

Chapter 8: Reconciling a Fractured Community

1. Since coming out of the theological closet back in 2011 and putting myself out there as a straight ally who is also a pastor from an evangelical background, this sort of thing happens often. I cherish it every time.

2. Specifically, Exodus International, the sham of an organization that acknowledged a couple years ago that people don't actually change their orientation.

3. Suetonius, and Catharine Edwards, *Lives of the Caesars* (Oxford: Oxford University Press, 2001), 184, 203.

4. Monumental to understanding Romans in this way is the work done on the "new perspective" of Paul by scholars like James Dunn and E. P. Sanders, expanded upon by the "fresh perspective" of NT Wright, and then further enlightened by the apocryphal studies of Douglas Campbell.

5. Aristotle, *Art of Rhetoric*, trans. J. H. Freese, Loeb Classical Library 193 (Cambridge, MA: Harvard University Press, 1926), 423.

6. Calvin Porter, "Romans 1:18–32: Its Role in the Developing Argument," *New Testament Studies* 40, no. 2 (1994): 223.

7. Porter, "Romans 1:18–32," 228.

8. For a fuller treatment on this perspective of Romans, where Paul bounces back and forth between his own thoughts and those of an imaginary sparring partner, see the game-changing work by Douglas Campbell on the book of Romans, *The Deliverance of God* (Grand Rapids: William B. Eerdmans, 2009).

9. Interestingly, in the Old Testament having long hair was seen as a virtue.

10. See chapter 6 in Matthew Vine's *God and the Gay Christian* for a full (and fascinating) treatment of this argument around "excess vs. moderation." Vine sees, as one of the primary issues at stake in Romans 1:26–27, men's lustful desire for excess. I don't disagree.

11. Augustine, *Answer to the Pelagians II: Marriage and Desire*, 20.35, ed. John E Rotelle, trans. Roland J. Teske (New York: New City Press, 1990), 75–76.

Chapter 9: Imagine a Church Where . . .

1. The domain www.churchofthedancingllamas.com is available, if you're interested.

2. This idea wasn't new to us. Jesus suggested it was the most important thing ever (see Matt. 22:37–39).

Chapter 10: Revisiting Forgotten Words

1. In a lovely twist of irony that even Alanis Morisette would appreciate, just six weeks after *UnClobber* came out, the Chicago Cubs did, in fact, win the World Series on November 2, 2016, putting to rest their 108 year losing streak and rendering my book obsolete almost immediately.

2. Remind me to keep her away from my five-year-old when he's building Legos, or she'll ask him to install her new washer and dryer.

3. According to the American Psychological Association, http://www.apa.org/helpcenter/sexual-orientation.aspx.

4. Pliny, *Natural History* 10, books 36–37, trans. D. E. Eichholz, Loeb Classical Library 419 (Cambridge, MA: Harvard University Press, 1962), 11:49.

5. Clement of Alexandria attributed this belief to the "followers of Basilides" in his *Stromata* 3.1.1, http://www.earlychristianwritings.com/text/clement-stromata-book3-english.html.

6. Gregory of Nazianzus, Oration 37.16, http://www.newadvent.org/fathers/310237.htm.

Afterword

1. Caryle Murphy, "Most U.S. Christian Groups Grow More Accepting of Homosexuality," Pew Research Center, https://www.pewresearch.org/fact-tank/2015/12/18/most-u-s-christian-groups-grow-more-accepting-of-homosexuality/.